THE COMMITTEE
FOR THE
REBURIAL
OF
LIVER-EATING
JOHNSTON

MEMOIRS OF A DYSLEXIC TEACHER

TRI ROBINSON

THE COMMITTEE

FOR THE

REBURIAL

OF

LIVER-EATING JOHNSTON

MEMOIRS OF A DYSLEXIC TEACHER

TRI ROBINSON

DEDICATION

*This true story of the reburial of John "Liver-eating" Johnston
will forever be indebted to the memory of Bob Edgar. A true
hero, not only because he did so many amazing things, but because
in humility, he dared to put faith in a bunch of junior high kids
who believed they could move the body of an old mountain man.*

~

*And to the memory of my old junior high teacher, Mr. Bill Hanson,
who not only believed in me but convinced me that I could one day
become a success. In so doing, he motivated me to eventually
become a junior high school teacher myself.*

TABLE OF CONTENTS

PREFACE

This is the true story of a seventh grade American Literature class who dug up and reburied the body of the legendary mountain man "Liver-eating" Johnston. The narrative provides a lively and inspiring historical account of the events and conflicts which surrounded Johnston's unorthodox disinterment from a veteran's cemetery in Southern California to his reburial in a historical cemetery in Cody, Wyoming.

After hearing of Johnston's romantic exploits as a mountain man in the Rocky Mountains, and discovering he was buried only a few hundred yards from the San Diego Freeway in the greater Los Angeles area, twenty-four students from Park View Junior High School in Lancaster, California, made the decision to move his remains back to the Big Sky country. Calling themselves "The Committee for the Reburial of Liver-eating Johnston" they spent the better part of a school year attempting to convince many others to join their efforts for the sake of gaining permission, financial support and the authority to disinter and move Johnston's decomposed body to a more fitting final resting place.

As chance would have it, the well-known Warner Bros. film, *Jeremiah Johnson*, starring Robert Redford, gained momentum in theaters across America the same year the class decided to move the Liver-eater's body. The film not only popularized Johnston's legendary life but helped generate public interest, aiding in the students' ultimate success.

This book is the story of the amazing quest that a class of twelve-year-olds dared to embrace. It is filled with many trials, miraculous encounters and the final victorious outcome. It reveals the conflict between two states that fought a political battle over Liver-eating Johnston's remains, each fighting for the right to provide his final burial place. It is the inspiring account of a group of spirited and courageous young people who dared to make right something they perceived as being very wrong – honoring the wishes of a dead man to be buried in the very land that had made him a legend. It includes the contributions of those such as Robert Redford and Roy Neil (NBC news correspondent who covered the Apollo lunar flights and landings in the 1960's), who both chose to back the act of a bunch of twelve-year-old kids.

"The Committee for the Reburial of Liver-eating Johnston" is a heartwarming story, humorous at times, which conveys a powerful message about what young people can accomplish when they put their minds and efforts towards something. It is a tale that affirms the effectiveness of innovative education and kinetic learning, and how a teacher's words of encouragement can empower and forever change a young person's life. And finally, it is the testimony of a tenacious group of junior high school students who discovered they could make a difference in their world when they chose to believe in themselves enough to try.

CHAPTER I

The Gift of a Teacher
Named Mr. Hanson

I n September of 1973 I was twenty-five years old and just beginning my second year of teaching in Lancaster, California. I was young and idealistic, believing that a teacher could change the world for the better, one student at a time. I believed this was true because of a teacher I encountered many years before who had not only empowered me, but showed me that teaching was more of a calling than a profession. Mr. Hanson was my seventh grade English teacher at Portola Junior High School in the San Fernando Valley of Southern California. He was a man who loved his classroom role and was made for it. He had the amazing ability to see through the exterior of his students into the inner qualities of their hearts and character. He saw things we couldn't see in ourselves, and by some miracle he saw something good in me.

Motivation for a Life of Teaching

In the early 1960's no one truly understood dyslexia. Today it is fairly common knowledge that it's a learning disability which

causes the brain to reverse the images of numbers and alpha-
betical letters making basic skills such as reading and spelling
next to impossible. For those like me, dyslexia created a hand-
icap that made a person, especially one just entering the seventh
grade, feel unintelligent and inadequate. Not a good thing for
a boy who was nearly the smallest in his class trying to survive
the basic feelings of inferiority that so often accompany adolescence. As a result, I hated school and spent most of my
classroom hours daydreaming of being in the mountains far
away. Hunting and fishing occupied my mind – two things I
was fairly good at for a boy my age.

One afternoon in the fall of my seventh grade year I was
called into the school counselor's office for what was supposed
to be an inspiring pep talk. It was a meeting prompted by another of my "not so great" report cards. I can't pretend to recall
the exact words Mrs. Jacobson said that day, but there were a
few things I never forgot. The conversation started out, as it
often did, with Mrs. Jacobson reminding me of my older sister
Gail's perfection. Gail had recently graduated to high school
with a 4.0 average and had been a gift to all her teachers. Mrs.
Jacobson also reminded me that my father, Dr. F. W. Robinson
Jr., was a highly respected high school principal in the same
school district. Neither of those realities was new to me; I lived
with both of those people and had great respect for them myself. I guess it was the context in which she framed her observations that stimulated an even greater awareness of my own
shortcomings. I couldn't help but compare my lack of academic
achievement with the reputations and accomplishments of so
many others who were in my life. The final clincher came when
Mrs. Jacobson asked to see my notebook.

In those days the commonly used notebook was a three-
ring binder covered with a blue denim material. At the beginning of every new school year students would be required to

organize dividers which had labeled tabs designating each class to be taken during the semester. One section would be designated for math, one for English, one for history, and so on. All assignments and homework pertaining to any given subject or class would be found in its proper place. That was good for the first few weeks of school, but a boy of thirteen who dreamed of hunting and fishing often neglected to keep things organized as well as they should be. Eventually homework assignments and other important papers had a way of getting stuck here and there, this way and that. In addition to this, the denim covers begged to be drawn on during moments of classroom doldrums, often becoming cluttered with squiggles and drawings of things like shotguns and fishing tackle. At any rate, when Mrs. Jacobson picked up my notebook she wasn't as careful as she might have been, causing the papers inside to go skittering across her desk and onto the floor. With that she said in a disgusted tone, "Franklin, (that's what I was called in those days) this notebook looks like your brains are going to look if you don't get your act together."

Then, intentionally driving the point home, she interjected, "If you don't start applying yourself at school, the only employment that will ever be available to you will be pumping gas."

At that moment I felt like a total loser. And, in retrospect some fifty years later, most gas stations have become self-service which would have rendered me completely and totally unemployable according to Mrs. Jacobson's admonitions. If I didn't get my act together, I was possibly destined to become a street person.

Not only did Mrs. Jacobson deliver a defeating and unempowering proclamation concerning my future, but to add insult to injury, she had actually verbalized the exact way I had privately been feeling about myself. I concluded she was right and hopelessly left her office, accepting her observations as total truth. What could be deemed as the worst day of my young life to that point, unbeknownst to me, would soon become one of the very best.

Transforming Words of a Caring Teacher

Emotionally limping back to Mr. Hanson's English class, I attempted to suck up my pain. The class was still in session so I quietly walked in and took my assigned seat, attempting to be as invisible as possible. Failing miserably at the effort, I must have exposed my dejected feelings with body language that any observant teacher could detect. When the release bell sounded, I found Mr. Hanson standing by my desk discreetly requesting me to stick around. I knew Mr. Hanson well. I knew he was a kind man. But, after the meeting I'd just experienced, my first thought was one of fear. I couldn't handle another scolding.

As the classroom emptied, Mr. Hanson sat on the desk adjacent to my own and began to speak. I can't recall all that he said, but I can say with absolute honesty that the heart of his message was a transforming moment in my young life. It served as a primer to ignite a long season of life change. He opened the conversation by telling me I was very smart and not stupid, as I had come to believe.

"Frank" he said, "I want to tell you something and I want you to believe me." He went on choosing his words carefully. "You have gifts that no one else has and when you fully discover them and start operating in them, you're going to become a great success. Your life is going to make a difference in this world if you stop believing lies about yourself, and if you don't give up." He spoke with certainty and authority. As I look back, knowing what I know now, his words were more like prophecy than hopeful thinking. He spoke of qualities in my character that were more important than academic deficiencies, telling me things about myself I couldn't imagine how he knew. He spoke about untapped gifts that had become suppressed and hidden beneath the surface of my inadequacies.

I'll never forget the twinkle in his eye when he said, "Frank, the only thing you'll need more than most others is two secretaries instead of one." I'll never forget that, because that, too, was a prophetic statement that would come to pass later in my life.

Mr. Hanson put his actions where his mouth was, offering to spend extra time with me. He taught me secrets concerning how to study and read. He taught me skills that would one day get me onto the dean's list with a Master's degree in Administrative Education. He did one other thing that day that may have had the most impact of all. He changed my name.

Up until then I had been called Franklin by my teachers at school and Frank by my close friends. I had always had the nickname "Tri" given to me by my parents. I was Franklin Willard Robinson III and "Tri" stood for three; like tricycle or triangle.

Mr. Hanson, making a play on words said, "From this day on we are going to call you 'Tri' instead of 'Frank' here at school because you will always have to remember to try just a little harder than everyone else." And so it was: I became known as Tri Robinson both socially and professionally from that day on.

Bad Things Can Be Used to Empower the Good

In the year before my conversation with Mr. Hanson some unfortunate events took place; events that I now believe set me up so that I would be ready to receive the full impact of his words that day. There's a scripture in the book of Romans that tells how God uses all things, even bad things, to turn our lives around for the good. It is sort of like that saying that goes; "No pain, no gain."

When I was in the sixth grade my parents thought I needed something to help build my self-esteem. The idea came to them that playing a musical instrument and becoming a part of the orchestra would be a good thing. I'm not sure how it was decided but within a matter of weeks I started taking flute lessons from a music teacher, Mr. Atkinson. He came faithfully to our home every Wednesday night right after dinner. He was a nice man and I suspect a good enough teacher, if his student had any musical ability at all. Unfortunately I wasn't the child prodigy my parents hoped for and I think Mr. Atkinson saw it right off. Nevertheless he continued to do his part preparing me to audition for the school orchestra the following semester. Surprising as it was for us all, and especially I think for Mr. Atkinson, I succeeded at the audition and was actually accepted.

One morning I rode my Schwinn bicycle to school after an overnight rain storm had soaked the streets. I was with a couple of buddies of mine, having a good time and probably not thinking too clearly. When I arrived at the school bike racks that morning I realized it was orchestra day and I had forgotten my flute. Things were bad enough at school as it was, and the thought of being ridiculed for yet another negligent memory loss was more than I could bear. In desperation and haste I made a last minute decision to make a run for home in hopes of retrieving the instrument and returning before the first period bell rang. I not only didn't make the bell that day, but didn't make it back to school for several weeks.

I jumped back on my cruiser and headed home as fast as I could peddle. Though the streets were slippery due to the rain, I threw all caution to the wind and rode as fast as I could until I rounded the final corner in front of our house. Going way too fast, I hit a mud-slick and skidded completely out of control. Not responding to my full pressure on the coaster brakes, the bike didn't slow down until it hit full-force into the front bumper of my mother's 1956 pink Cadillac. The impact catapulted me head first into the air. I bounced like a flat rock skipping off the car's metal roof before touching down mouth-first in the gutter on the opposite side. The impact hurt, but I had survived; at least I thought I had, until my tongue felt the strange sensation of an empty hole where all of my front teeth once had been. They were mysteriously gone and the reality of it took only a few seconds to register. This new revelation motivated a spontaneous death curdling scream which my mother easily heard at the far end of our house. It was the kind of scream that takes years off a mother's life, especially when she sees blood streaming from her child's mouth. It was a bad day for my mom, and an even worse day for me.

Going back to that afternoon in Mr. Hanson's classroom, I want to summarize the events surrounding my life and why his timely words had such a lasting impact. First, I was in the heat of adolescence, the most awkward season of the human experience. Second, my name was "Franklin"; and not just Franklin, but "Franklin Willard Robinson III". Third, I was the smallest boy in my grade with the exception of one other kid. Fourth, I had dyslexia which made me feel extremely stupid at the time. And finally, I played the flute, or at least I did until I knocked out all my front teeth. I might add that knocking my teeth out resulted in a fairly messed up face for quite awhile. All of this to say at that moment in my life, I was completely and totally convinced that I was the biggest loser in my school, and possibly in the entire human race.

Mr. Hanson chose secondary education more as a life calling than a profession because of a deep desire to help kids like me succeed. In the coming weeks he lived up to his promise and invited me to stay after school. He didn't require or demand it, but offered his extra time to teach me how to beat the system. By that I mean he showed me how to get the most out of a chapter in a textbook without reading it in its entirety. He introduced me to things like Cliff Notes and other shortcut methods for retaining information and successfully taking tests.

He had assured me that I would have no trouble getting ahead in life because of my personality and willingness to work. Then he told me something I couldn't believe; he told me I was a leader, and in time I'd see people wanting to follow me. That was one thing I didn't see in myself, but in just a few years I became the captain of both my track and cross country teams in high school. These were teams that won city championships in the Los Angeles school system two years in a row. Later in life I became recognized nationally as school teacher of the year. And after retiring early from a teaching profession, I founded and built a church of over 2,000 people and became a leader in our international church movement. No one could have been more surprised than I was as my life of leadership unfolded over the next fifty years. Sometimes I wonder if Mr. Hanson didn't speak these things into existence. I have learned over the years that words are very powerful; either blessings or curses that carry with them the ability to build people up or tear them down.

My dad became the principal of Beverly Hills High School and was recognized as one of the top administrative educators in the United States. This probably had an impact on my later decision to enter the field of education. In retrospect, I think it was more because of my relationship with Mr. Hanson that in my second year of teaching, I found myself entering a seventh grade classroom full of gifted but unmotivated students at Park View Junior High School in Lancaster, California. I wanted to help young people see their greater potential, even when they couldn't see it in themselves. I wanted to do for others what Bill Hanson had done for me.

First Year of Teaching – Park View Junior High School
My first year of teaching began in 1972 and it was a wonderful and rich experience. I discovered I really loved teaching. Along

with loving what you do, creativity and imagination are probably the next biggest keys to a teacher's success. I found that
kids responded to teachers who were willing to put aside stale
lesson plans with a readiness to take a few risks and break status
quo. Looking back I think one of the main motivations that
drove me into the teaching profession was a desire to keep my
classroom creative and alive because of my own personal struggles in school. I wanted to prove that a student could learn and
actually thrive in the process.

Towards the end of my first year I received a notice from
our school principal, Dr. Dwight Stapley, requesting me to
come to his office. I was nervous about the unexpected meeting
because I knew some of the things I had done to liven up my
classroom had been a bit unconventional and had irritated a
few of the teachers on staff. For example, when I fired off my
old .50 caliber Hawkins muzzle-loading rifle outside the door
of my classroom (with a blank, of course – I'm not crazy), I
knew right away it wasn't the best idea. The students loved it
and it did add flavor to an otherwise mundane lesson on the
Civil War. But it drew quite a few scowls as several teachers
peered out their doors down the corridor. Also, I had already
been pulled into the principal's office for a reprimand which
turned out to be a simple but very bad misunderstanding.

That particular time Dr. Stapley had called me into his office and asked me to take a seat. I could tell by his actions that
what was about to take place was going to be uncomfortable
for him, and most likely for me as well. Dwight liked me, I
knew that much. But, I also knew something was up and I had
the distinct feeling it wasn't going to be good. He started by
telling me he had received a complaint from an irate mother
of one of my students. My wheels immediately started to turn.
What had I done most recently to merit the words "irate
mother"? I couldn't pull up anything. Then he told me. He said

it straight out, "A mother called me this morning extremely upset because she saw you in a local department store yesterday afternoon. She said she saw you holding hands with one of your students."

Wow! When he said that, I totally freaked out. "What!" I said, "With what student?"

"She didn't give a name" he said, "but did mention that she was really cute."

My wheels started to turn again only a little more rapidly now. "Are you sure she said it was me?" I asked.

With sternness in his voice, Dr. Stapley said that the mother was absolutely certain it was me. My reaction to this whole declaration, both with words and a bright red face, must have convinced him of my guilt. I hesitated before saying anything else. My personal calendar and schedule started turning around and around in my head. Where had I been yesterday afternoon; had I been in that store at all? Suddenly it hit me; yes I had been there. Not with a student, but with my wife, Nancy! Both the humor and relief of the revelation came out in a huge outburst of laughter. Dwight must have been bewildered and mystified as he waited for the explanation of my uncanny response.

I burst out with great relief, "That wasn't a student, that was my wife." Nancy, twenty-one at the time, had always looked young for her age and was no doubt, very cute. But, my students were twelve years old for goodness sake! I might also add, in those days twelve-year-old girls actually looked like they were twelve years old.

Dwight and I had a good laugh, but later that night when I told Nancy what had occurred the only thing she said was, "Looking twelve years old is not a compliment!" This was especially true considering she was pregnant with our first child. As for me, I still thought it was funny.

I was a little nervous when Principal Stapley asked for another visit. His secretary showed me into his office and I took a seat anticipating at least a mild scolding for something I probably deserved. To my great relief, the rebuke I had braced for never came. Instead he offered me the opportunity to take a new position the following year. He offered me the position to teach in what was called the GATE Program. GATE was an acronym for "Gifted and Talented Education", a special class for kids who had been identified and categorized as potentially high achievers. This didn't mean that they were high achievers, just that they had the potential. In fact, many of them had become so bored with school they had a tendency to be disruptive in class. They were sometimes known for using their smarts to terrorize teachers. They had been unmotivated, unchallenged and disillusioned with status quo, standardized, textbook teaching. What they needed was to be challenged or, as it was stated in the manual I later studied on the matter, the GATE program required the students to receive *"quantitative, differentiated curriculum"*. Simply put, they needed a more stimulating and creative learning environment than they might encounter in the conventional classroom. The biggest advantage to this new assignment was that it would grant me greater freedom as the teacher. It would encourage me to look for ways of teaching students away from the school campus, if and when it was applicable to the curriculum. Honestly, this was music to my ears.

A significant point concerning the story I'm about to tell as it relates to the reburial of Liver-eating Johnston is that one of the classes I would be assigned to teach was "American History and Literature". Again, looking back, I feel that this was just another piece of a great plan. Needless to say I took the position even though I had deep reservations that the kids I would be encountering could both read and spell circles around me. I could feel my old fears and insecurities rising up.

Even after five successful years of college and a year of teaching under my belt, I still hadn't completely overcome my personal learning disabilities. I had learned how to compensate for my dyslexia issue, but truth be known, it was still privately at work whittling away at my self-confidence. If one of my classes was going to be English Literature, you would think the teacher should at least be able to write on the chalk board (we did use chalk boards in those days) without having the fear of misspelling words. What great laughs that could bring from a class full of kids who, it was said, would be looking for some devious way to humiliate and take down the teacher. The very thought was enough to keep me awake at night even though I had already said "yes" to the challenge.

At times like this I would find myself returning to the counsel of Mr. Hanson for strength and direction. I recall him telling me that in order to be a success I would need to reach deep for creativity and learn to compensate by drawing on my strengths rather than allowing my weaknesses to dominate the outcome of my actions. One of my strengths was storytelling. Another was in the area of history, literature and folklore of the old West. If there is one thing five years of university work did for me, it was to give me a deep love and appreciation for the history and literature of the old West. And so it was there that I would go for strength.

As my teaching experience unfolded at Park View Junior High School, I soon realized a very important truth. I discovered that every student, whether struggling with disabilities as I had, or participating in a gifted and talented program, would need a Mr. Hanson in their life.

CHAPTER 2

First Awakenings to the Legend and Life of Liver-eating Johnston

The College of Idaho and Professor Dr. Louie Attebery

I entered College of Idaho in 1966, five years before I was hired as a teacher in the Lancaster School District. I was accepted on academic probation because I had never completed a foreign language in high school due to my ongoing struggle with dyslexia. My first two years of college were very difficult even though I used every method of compensation my old teacher Mr. Hanson had taught me. My professors seemed to like me because they knew how hard I tried. Because the college was small, only 1,000 students at the time, they were willing to invest in my progress. There was one class I dreaded having to take more than all the others; one I simply couldn't avoid. American Literature was a general requirement for all undergraduate work and as you might assume, requires reading, and lots of it. Up until this time I had only read one book cover

23

to cover in my entire life. It was a great book, too. It was called *Sand* and was written by Will James, one of the first great western authors. The old western term, "sand", stood for guts or courage. The story told the tale of a man who, knowing nothing of the western ways, managed to capture and break a beautiful wild stallion in the canyons of Arizona purely due to his own fortitude and "sand". It was the story of a person overcoming his fears and doing amazing things because of that. And, I might add, winning the beautiful girl in the end. That story was another life lesson for a young man who needed to learn to pursue his own aspirations with sand.

Even entrance into Dr. Louie Attebery's *Literature of the American West* class was a hurdle that I dreaded facing. If there had been any way to dodge that class I would have surely taken it. But if I had, I would have missed one of the great blessings of my life. Dr. Attebery loved the American West, and the first book he assigned in his class to be read was a trilogy written by the author A. B. Guthrie: *The Big Sky, The Way West* and *These Thousand Hills.* They were delightfully written, telling the story of three distinct eras of western development. All of the books were set in the Big Sky Country, a territory which included the three states of Idaho, Montana and Wyoming.

Discovering the Legend of John "Liver-eating" Johnston
Knowing I needed a head start on such a challenge I went straight back to my dorm room and opened the first book, *The Big Sky.* From the very first page my imagination exploded. It took me back to the early 1800's, a time when the land was undefiled from the onslaught of development that would soon change it forever. I dreamed of fur trapping, of hunting with a muzzle-loading rifle, eating fresh buffalo meat and of endless discovery. As I read, I longed to have lived at a time when the rivers ran free and men could sustain life with a good knife, a flintlock rifle and a spirit of adventure. One page led to the

next and before I realized it, I had finished the first book and was reading the second, and then the third. All at once it struck me; I could read! I wasn't fast, but I was persistent and I quickly found that the secret to learning to read was simply to read. When I finished Guthrie's trilogy I was hungry for more and considered scheduling a meeting with Dr. Attebery to see if he had more reading recommendations.

One morning I stopped by the Student Union between classes for a quick cup of coffee, which wasn't unusual in itself. What was unusual was that as I entered the coffee shop I spotted Dr. Attebery sitting alone at a table reading the morning paper. I'd never spoken to him one-on-one before and felt a little intimidated to interrupt his morning solitude. I did have a legitimate question to ask and because I intended to meet with him anyway, I sucked up my insecurity and approached his table. "Dr. Attebery," I said, "My name is Tri Robinson and I was wondering if I could ask you a question?"

He looked up at me. "Hi Tri," he said. "I know who you are, and of course you can ask me anything you want. What is it?" The tone of his voice immediately put me at ease.

"Well," I said, now with a little more confidence, "I just finished Guthrie's trilogy and really enjoyed it." I couldn't tell if he had any idea how great a victory it had been for me to have successfully read three books in a row. If so, he didn't let on.

"Great," he responded, "What did you like about them? I mean, specifically what part?" I told him I really enjoyed *The Big Sky* most of all. It was the book that dealt with the trapper/mountain man era, telling the story of a fictitious character named Boone Caudill.

"Well" he said, "Are you ready for more?"

"Yes, I am!" I said, "But, I don't know where I could find another book as captivating as those were."

He chuckled and replied, "Oh, don't you worry."

I could tell he was pleased. I didn't know if it was because he found a student who was reading for the joy of it instead of an obligation to a mandatory assignment, or because he shared my same interests. But he visibly lit up.

"Right offhand I'll tell you about two other books I think you'll really enjoy. Both are written by one of my favorite Idaho authors, Vardis Fisher. The first is called *Tale of Valor*. It's a novelized account of the Lewis and Clark expedition. The second is a book called *Mountain Man*. It's much like *The Big Sky*, but it's based on a real historical person. Oh, I'd have to say Fisher took a lot of poetic license by changing the character's name and romanticizing his life some, but the story is actually based on a person who became known all over the Big Sky region as 'Liver-eating Johnston'."

That was the first time I had ever heard of anyone named Liver-eating Johnston, but the idea of it fascinated me. Thanking Dr. Attebery, I went into the college bookstore on my way out of the student union building and immediately purchased both books.

I thoroughly enjoyed *Tale of Valor*, the story of the Lewis and Clark expedition. In fact, I still have a hard copy of it on my bookshelf today. The second book, *Mountain Man,* captured my imagination. It was, as Dr. Attebery said, a fascinating account of a true historical character that became a legend even in his own day. Johnston was a 260 pound frontiersman, as well as a trapper, logger, military scout and Indian fighter. His real name was John Johnston; some said his middle name was Jeremiah which may have inspired the title of the 1972 movie, *Jeremiah Johnson*. That movie wouldn't be released for another five years from the time I met with Dr. Attebery.

Jeremiah Johnson was a Warner Bros. production starring Robert Redford. The most amazing thing is that the movie would debut around the same time I was assigned the position to teach in the GATE program in Southern California. Something important that should be noted at this juncture of my story is that the true historical character of John "Liver-eating" Johnston spelled his last name with a "t", while the creators of the movie, *Jeremiah Johnson*, for reasons of their own, dropped the "t" from his name. I say this so as not to bring confusion as my story continues.

After reading Vardis Fisher's book, I became intrigued with this man, John Johnston, and was eager to learn more about him. I discovered a second book about his life called *Crow Killer* by Raymond Thorp and Robert Bunker. This book was said to be more historically accurate than Fisher's account as it connected fiction and legend with historical fact concerning Johnston's life. It told the story in greater detail concerning the death of Johnston's Indian wife and unborn child, and how he had blamed the Crow Indian Nation for their murders. According to the account he had a one-man vendetta against every Crow warrior he could hunt down. The story went that his fighting continued for fifteen years until a time when he finally decided to bury the hatchet (and not in some poor Indian's head), for the sake of making peace with the Crow Nation. In the end he became respected and embraced by the tribe. Going through many other historical accounts of Johnston's exploits, most of this legend is passed off as folklore. The more I read, the more I found it difficult to separate historical truth from romantic legend. In the end it didn't really matter to me; I simply loved reading the books.

Johnston's story led me to dozens of other books telling the true life adventures of many iconic frontiersmen. Men like John Colter who, after leaving the Lewis and Clark expedition in 1804, was captured by the Blackfeet Indians at the headwaters of the Missouri River. Based on Colter's personal account, the Indians stripped him naked including his moccasins and told him to run for his life. He did so and was pursued by a dozen fearsome warriors who intended to kill him for sport. Mile after mile he ran, managing to kill one Indian with his own lance. In a total state of extreme exhaustion he arrived at the banks of the Gallatin River where he took refuge inside a beaver lodge and hid until nightfall. When the coast was finally clear Colter made an amazing trek, walking naked for 200 miles. It was half way across what is today known as the state of Montana. After many days of hunger and exposure he arrived at Fort Raymond, a trapper's outpost on the Yellowstone River. He had only eaten bark and roots to avoid starvation.

Another frontiersman, Hugh Glass, was an early member of the Rocky Mountain Fur Company. Glass was a hunter and trapper who was mauled by a grizzly bear and left for dead by three companions. He is best known for his historical journey, crawling with deep lacerations and a badly broken leg across what is now North Dakota. And there was also Jedediah Smith, the first to journey all the way to California, crossing the southern deserts and surviving three of the worst Indian massacres of that time period. Maybe the most famous of all mountain men was Jim Bridger. He was considered one of the greatest leaders during the trapping era. Then there was Kit Carson, who seemed to be afraid of nothing though he only stood 5' 5" and weighed a mere 140 pounds. No man knew the trails of the western United States during the mid-1800s like Carson did; thus he was requisitioned to be the main scout for the famous Freemont expeditions. Carson was responsible for the discovery of many new mountain passes and routes which later enabled wagon trains to navigate west. This brought the opening of new trails all the way to Oregon and California, thus starting the westward migration of miners and homesteaders.

The list went on and on, and with every character there

was a book begging to be read. I read and read until I literally was healed of a weakness that very well could have robbed me of the life of fulfillment I later experienced as a teacher. In some ways you might say, as ironic as it might sound, Liver-eating Johnston and his contemporaries were used as agents for healing in my life. They enabled me to grow into the educator I was destined to become.

A Mountain Man's Breakfast for Attebery

Living on campus in a men's dorm during my first two years of college gave me the opportunity to make a couple of very good friends, Johnny Bingham and Don Peterson. As the three of us started our junior year, however, we decided to rent a rundown, back-alley apartment we fondly named "The Cabin". The Cabin was located about two blocks from campus and it provided a whole new level of freedom for three young men who were ready to be on their own. We had no curfews and no rules. We could come and go as we pleased; and we did.

All of us had been in Dr. Attebery's literature class and had read the same books, which undoubtedly influenced the way we decorated The Cabin. In the main room, (living room, kitchen and dining room) we hung animal hides on the walls, and placed a large cowhide on the floor as a throw rug. By the door there was a large brass spittoon. Old lever action Winchester rifles and shotguns were also used as décor along with beaver traps, a powder horn and other odds and ends of western memorabilia. In the center of the room was an old ornate claw-foot bathtub; its main function was to hold ice and Friday night beverages. Off to one side stood a classic oak table with a lion foot pedestal, which none of us fully appreciated at the time. I owned a very large Bowie style hunting knife which we often used to butcher the rewards of our hunting trips. Not having proper respect for the table, my knife was often found buried tip first in its top. All three of us developed a deep love for the Idaho backcountry and spent many free weekends hunting deer, elk, ducks and pheasants. We loved to explore the Idaho wilderness and climb its mountain peaks together. For us, it was a truly rich and memorable season of life, and The Cabin expressed our passion for all things *Idaho* – the great outdoors and the rich western history.

One day we came up with the idea of inviting Dr. Attebery for a real Idaho breakfast. We had just shot a deer and thought preparing a meal for him would be a good way to thank him for the great experience we all had in his class. We had no idea if he'd come, but decided to give it a try and sent him an invitation. The Cabin had a bit of a reputation, some of which was not all that respectable, and because our perspective of him was one of dignity and respect, we weren't all that sure he'd accept the invitation. To our amazement and elation, he not only accepted but asked what he could bring to contribute to the meal. More excited than ever, we all jumped in and started planning the menu.

We gleaned potatoes out of a field not too far from town; cut thick slabs of steak off the deer haunch; and prepared every other kind of wild meat we had in our meat locker. We had been nurturing a sourdough starter in those days and used it to griddle up a mountain of very sour pancakes, steaming hot with real butter and maple syrup. It was an authentic mountain man feast for sure. Dr. Attebery showed up with homemade huckleberry preserves made from berries he and his wife had picked in the hills. The table was set and ready with my great Bowie knife serving as a centerpiece stuck in the middle. We ate and talked for several hours, telling story after story about our adventures. During our breakfast together, we discovered a side of Louie Attebery we hadn't known before.

That day Dr. Attebery became not only a respected and much loved professor, but also a lifelong friend. I have bumped into him several times through the years, and he never forgot my name or the meal we shared together. In May of 2008, at sixty years old, I was asked to come back to the College of Idaho to speak at that year's graduation. To my surprise I was presented with the President's Medallion. It was an honor bestowed once a year to an alumnus who had used their education to contribute something of value to society. The large metal medallion was presented to me by the college president, and also to my great pleasure, Dr. Attebery, who had retired from classroom teaching but still served on the college's board of trustees.

Who would have guessed back in the late 1960's that a kid who almost didn't make it past his second year of college would receive such an honor? Dr. Attebery and a handful of committed teachers including Mr. Hanson became powerful influencers in my life. Their passion and guidance set me on a trajectory towards a life of following in their footsteps, teaching and influencing others, both young and old.

CHAPTER 3

Meeting Bob Edgar - Founder of
"Old Trail Town" Cody, Wyoming

Getting Acquainted with Johnston's Life and Legend

I completed my undergraduate work at the College of Idaho in 1969 with a major in physical education. I chose P.E. because of a dream I had of one day becoming a high school track and cross-country coach. I then entered the Master's program majoring in administrative education, which opened up new horizons and influenced my future aspirations. A requirement for my master's work was to write a dissertation or thesis. Because of my newfound love for western history I chose to write my paper on the Big Sky Country. Yet, because of my lingering fear of high level academia, I dreaded the idea of attempting to complete a lengthy technical dissertation on the history of a geographical region. It sounded mundane for someone like me, so I proposed a unique idea to the professor who had been assigned as my thesis advisor. My proposal was this: to combine the teaching and administrative skills I had been taught through the Master's program with the value for kinetic education, which I had learned in my undergraduate physical education classes. I decided to develop a creative curriculum that was both cognitive and kinetic. That is to say, it would include educational information, but would require physical activity as a part of the learning process. I proposed to develop an educational travel guide to be used while students were on a fifteen-day bicycle tour through the Big Sky states. The route I chose would follow seven different historical trails including the Oregon/California Trail, the Coulter Trial, the Bozeman Trail and a portion of the Lewis and Clark Trail. As participants engaged in the tour they would receive college credits in the subjects of western history, literature, folklore and physical education. Simply stated, it would be a lecture class on wheels. My proposed route transcended several hundred miles of beautiful country starting in Soda Springs, Idaho, then passing through Jackson Hole, Wyoming, and Yellowstone National Park. The route then descended eastward into Cody, Wyoming, and circled back crossing southern Montana. It would pass through the famous Three Forks region of western Montana, following Lewis and Clark's route over the Continental Divide into Idaho. The trip would end in Lemhi Valley where the Expedition met Sacajawea's Shoshone tribe before their final quest through the Rocky Mountains and on to the Pacific Ocean.

Naturally, one thing I had to do before writing such a paper would be to take the tour myself. Nancy and I had just been married so we decided to take the journey together, making it more like a vacation. We carried bikes on the back of our 1965 VW Bug so we could transport research and writing materials as well as food and camping equipment. Most of the time Nancy followed me in the car while I rode stretches of the route on my bike. We camped at night in public campgrounds and during the day met with people who could help with my research along the route. It was on one of those days that we met Bob Edgar for the first time.

Bob was an archeologist and historian known for his commitment to preserve old historic structures which he located, disassembled and reconstructed in a location on the outskirts of Cody, Wyoming. It was a place he called "Old Trail Town". From the first time we met I really liked Bob. He was a soft-spoken man, very humble in nature, but obviously a person of great depth. He was not only known as an archeologist and historian but an author and artist. He was about ten years older than I was and it didn't take long to discover that he had gained a world of knowledge in that time; knowledge I needed to complete my thesis.

My research had revealed that Johnston spent a good deal of time around the Cody area. Especially in his later years he had visited many hot springs that were very near the present site of Old Trail Town. It was called Colter's Hell. The hot bubbling water rising out of the Shoshone River had been visited by John Colter in the winter of 1807-08. He later described it to Captain Clark when he returned to civilization. I asked Bob for more details about when Johnston visited the hot springs.

"Yeah," he said, "Johnston hung out in these parts, especially when he got a bad case of arthritis as an older man." He went on, "in his later years the rugged mountain life was getting difficult; especially after sleeping so many cold nights in the rain and snow, and wading in icy cold streams to fish out traps. He figured he needed a more civilized life and decided to settle down in Red Lodge, just north of here about sixty miles. He became the town constable for several years there and was known all over this country. Mothers used to tell their kids when they'd been bad that if they didn't straighten up, old Johnston would come and eat their liver. That was one thing that made his legendary name stick."

"Anyway," Bob continued, "Johnston used to spend a lot

of time right down there in the Shoshone River sitting in the hot sulfur water of Colter's Hell, soaking his old weary bones."

"Very interesting," I responded. "It seemed to me I read somewhere that he was at one time a military scout in the Wyoming country. Is that true?"

"Oh yes," he said. "He was a scout for General Miles Nelson because at that time he not only knew the country better than most men, but also the ways of the Indians. He was fearless when it came to Indians."

"By the way," he added, "according to military records his real name was John Garrison Johnston." That was news to me, since some had been saying his middle name was Jeremiah, even before the movie had been released.

My conversation with Bob concerning Johnston went on for a long time. He knew more about Johnston's life than anyone I'd met. Bob and I became good friends for the next few years and once spent a day together walking the hills, shooting our old muzzle loader rifles together. He would place large sheets of white slate rock in the limbs of trees and we'd shoot them, watching our .50 caliber balls shatter them into small fragments.

At first impression, Old Trail Town may have appeared to be just a tourist stop on the side of the highway. Upon closer examination, it was revealed to be a non-profit museum consisting of authentic historic buildings. On the premises Bob had reassembled historic western structures such as the original Bucket of Blood Saloon and the Butch Cassidy Hole in the Wall Cabin. Bob had made Old Trail Town a special place because of his passion for the old west, and his reputation for living the history he loved. Among other things Bob was known as a true artist with a Colt 45 pistol. He had such a reputation of excellence with his pistol that people who knew him would often let him shoot out the ace of spades on a playing card while holding it in their fingers from a distance of forty paces. He was also known to shoot cigarettes out of his wife's mouth at the county fair every summer until stress in their marital relationship eventually put an end to it.

Bob immediately caught the value of what I was trying to accomplish with my Master's project and volunteered to help out any way he could. This started a valuable working relationship between us; one that would eventually involve his participation in my seventh grade class several years later.

A Bear Story I Never Forgot

Once I was with Bob on an errand, driving through Yellowstone National Park. While passing through the park we were stopped by a "bear jam". This traffic jam is caused by tourists stopping to watch bears on the side of the road. Seeing a large mother grizzly bear with her two half grown cubs inspired the telling of bear stories. I had a few stories of my own from my hunting days in Idaho, but the story he told me topped all others. He shared an encounter with me that he had a number of years before. It was a story that I'd never forget.

While guiding a hunting party in the Yellowstone wilderness Bob unexpectedly came upon a huge grizzly bear feeding on entrails from an elk Bob had field dressed earlier in the day. He told me he returned to the site where he had hoped to catch a fur bearing animal feeding on the carcass. He said in those days he didn't make a lot of money as a hunting guide and often sold coyote or bobcat hides for extra income. He had ridden his horse to within a quarter mile of the site. He dismounted and began quietly sneaking through the woods with pistol in hand. He told me the snow was two feet deep and trying to negotiate deadfall aspen trees while staying as stealth as possible was a challenge. When he got within pistol range of the elk's remains he crouched down having spotted movement in the fallen trees and brush before him. All at once a massive boar grizzly stood up on his hind legs, sniffing the air and spotting

Bob. Quickly assessing the situation, Bob realized he couldn't outrun the bear, and there were no trees large enough to climb out of reach. At that moment he knew he was a dead man. He had no rifle with him; his only source of defense was his Colt pistol. A Colt 45 is a large pistol, no doubt, but not big enough to boost your confidence when confronted by a huge grizzly who believes you are encroaching on his dinner. As the bear was about to charge, Bob made a snap decision to shoot him in the chest. He used four of his six shots, knowing that he hit his target. Yet, this only made the bear more irate. For a moment the huge animal clawed at his wounds while still focusing his attention on his attacker. Bob knew he had lost his only hope for escape and was preparing himself for the worst when an amazing thing occurred that saved his life.

In shock and disbelief Bob watched as a second bear, nearly as large as the first, rose up accompanied by two half-grown cubs. It was an entire bear family! But instead of coming after Bob, the male bear turned on the mother bear and her cubs. In his pain he attacked his own family. Bob told me he had never heard such clamor as the entire clan entered into a massive bear fight. Bob seized the moment and quickly fled back through the trees to his horse and returned to camp without haste. He returned to the site the next day to find the dead male bear. The area where the fight had occurred looked as if a bomb had gone off; trees were flattened and there was blood and fur strewn everywhere.

Not only have I never forgotten Bob's bear story, but during my later years of ministry I often used it as an illustration when teaching about marriage and family crisis. The story served as a perfect example of how families are destroyed when a father or husband responds to their personal pain by attacking the wrong people. Rather than addressing the real source of their emotional pain, many men often attack and abuse the very ones they love and are called to protect. It was a vivid picture of a tragedy that unfortunately befalls many families all too often. Bob never knew it, but his bear story was instrumental in bringing healing to many broken and damaged relationships in a way he could have never guessed.

All I have shared about Bob reveals who he really was; a true western man with many life adventures which gave him not only the knowledge of western ways, but the reputation for knowing what he was talking about. He was not an armchair historian, but rather a person whose real life resembled many of those I read about in the books my old professor recommended. As for me and the twenty-four students at Park View School that I later had the privilege of teaching, Bob Edgar was a true hero. Not only because he did so many amazing things, but because in humility, he dared to put faith in a bunch of junior high kids who believed they could move the body of an old mountain man.

Returning to California:
Settling on Our Family's Old Homestead

I will be forever grateful for knowing men like Louie Attebery and Bob Edgar, whose passion for the history and lore of the Rocky Mountains inspired and challenged me. Without their influence in my life, I might never have discovered the richness of learning about American legends like Johnston. And having the opportunity to live in Idaho during my college years gave me the vision and expertise to pursue the profession of teaching. With a newfound love for the history and wilderness of Idaho, Nancy and I hoped we could continue to live there. But, the timing for that was not right yet. There was important work for us to do first in California.

We left Idaho as a young couple, accepting an offer from my parents to move onto our family's old homestead near the Tehachapi Mountains in Southern California. The old ranch had been in our family for four generations, used only as a hunting cabin for many years. Some of the best times of my childhood had been at the ranch, and because Nancy was willing, we went for it. We left Idaho in December of 1971, driving our Volkswagen Bug more than 800 miles south. We moved onto the small ranch right before Christmas. There was three feet of snow at the time so we had to pack all our belongings from the county road up the mountain about a quarter mile. Thankfully, my dad had cut and stacked firewood before the big snow fell. That was a blessing since the only source of heat in the small, uninsulated cabin was an open fireplace in the living area and my great-grandmother's wood cook stove in the kitchen. The place had spring-fed water running into the cabin, but no electricity and no phone. It was rugged, but an exciting adventure for two newlyweds who were happy to spend the winter snuggling on the couch in front of the fire.

We worked on the little homestead throughout the following spring and summer, restoring it as best we could with what little money we had. We cleared the land, planted our first vegetable garden, and established an orchard. I dug a root cellar to store and preserve Nancy's canning and fixed up an old outbuilding to use as a workshop. I hunted for much of our food in the surrounding hills and butchered the meat myself. We were living out our dream, but because you can't live on dreams, we soon realized it was time for me to seek a real job. The closest town of any size was Lancaster, about an hour's drive down from the mountain. I was hired on by the Lancaster School District as a secondary teacher for Park View Junior High School. Years of preparation, some of which reached all the way back to my own junior high school experiences, had equipped and prepared me for this new season of life; a season as a professional educator. And so it is that the story I'm telling really begins.

CHAPTER 4

The First Day of School – September 1973

The Roll Call

On the first day of school at eight o'clock one Monday morning, it started. The tardy bell rang and twenty-four seats in my new classroom were occupied with twelve- and thirteen-year-old students. Some resembled a deer in the headlights while others seemed far too confident for their own good and mine. No matter, they were there ready to hear what their new teacher had to offer, and what was in store for the next nine months of their lives. One thing every experienced teacher understands is that the first day of school has a way of setting precedence for the remainder of the entire semester. If the first day goes poorly, especially when working with junior high students, the rest of the semester can easily become a disaster. The first day has a way of launching the attitude and atmosphere of the class on a course that will either take it on a positive or negative journey. Because of this fairly well-known truth, there are several different strategies teachers commonly apply. The first is the "authoritarian dictator" approach. It's true, the classroom was never meant to be a democracy, but when the word tyranny comes to mind, it may be a bit much. These teachers start off with a countenance of being really tough, setting rules and establishing mandates with a harsh, no-compromise tone to their voice that communicates, "Don't even think of messing with me." On the other end of the spectrum is the teacher that tries to act more like a peer; being witty and friendly with an attitude which communicates, "I'm just one of you and we can all be really good pals." Those teachers are generally screaming like babies by the end of the first week, if not sooner. As for me, I took the middle approach. I decided to take roll call.

Because I would be teaching American Literature and History, I decided to bring in a weathered 1800's vintage saddle from my tack room at the ranch. I set it on a saddle tree in the front of my classroom. I used it for atmosphere and as a teaching podium. I perched myself on a barstool to one side of it and started taking roll. This would normally be the job of my student aide, but that day I wanted to use roll call as a means of making a short personal connection with each student.

I methodically started; "Julie Aden," I called out.

A quiet shy sounding voice from the left side of the room said, "Here."

"Hi Julie," I said. "How are you today?"

"Fine, thank you." she responded hesitantly.

"Did you have a good summer, Julie?" I asked.

"Yes, Mr. Robinson," she mumbled quietly.

"What did you do?" I said it in a way to let her know I actually cared. I think it caught her off guard as I waited a minute for a reply.

Then quite shyly she replied, "I don't know; just stuff."

I moved on, not wanting to embarrass her. I called the next name on the class roll. "Danette Appier?"

"Here," came a second response.

I looked up, making eye contact and asked, "How about you, Danette; did you have a good summer?"

"It was okay," she responded.

"Do you like history, Danette?" I asked.

"Not too much," she said quietly.

I looked at her, feeling sorrow over her comment. "I'm sorry for that. I really do hope we can change that this semester."

She didn't say anything but smiled a very sweet smile. I smiled back and went on.

"Kif Anderson," I called.

This time a stronger more confident voice came back in response, "Right here, Mr. Robinson."

"Hi Kif!" I said; "How about you, what did you do this summer?"

"I worked on some new magic tricks," he said. Then, without taking a breath, Kif went on to tell me and the rest of the class all about what he had learned, offering to show us a few things. I told him we'd all love to see his skill but we'd have to wait for a better time.

The list continued for the next fifteen or twenty minutes. It was a long roll call, but at the end I knew I was going to really love this group of kids. I felt a kind of warmth for them and a connection which was unusual on the first day of school. The fears that had built up in my mind because of the warnings I'd received earlier had dissipated. I knew right then it was going to be a special year, though I had no idea what that would look like.

Unbeknownst to any of us, the list of names I read that day would be recorded in the Congressional Records of the United States 93rd Congress only nine months later on June 27th, 1974. The list would be followed by the words of the

Honorable William Ketchum, representative for the State of California. It read, *"Mr. Speaker, I would like to share with my colleagues an account of a recent event which illustrates the character and spirit of American's youth… I know my colleagues join me in commending Mr. Robinson and his students for the integral role they played in the re-burial of Jeremiah Johnson. It reflects pride in our nation's heritage. I am honored to submit their names for your information with deep appreciation for a job well done on behalf the historical figure Jeremiah Johnson."* The letter then listed all twenty-four of the students who were sitting in my class that first day. They are listed here in the order they appeared in the Congressional Record:

Julia Aden
Danette Appier
Kif Anderson
Becky Carey
Kelly Daugherty
Tami Downing
Kirk Dowsett
Mark Endures
Jerry Fields
Ron Flores
Monica Garza
Russell Gilliam
Nancy Goldsworthy
Kevin Jennings
Paul Kiyono
Ron Langley
Keith Marshall
Pat McIver
Lia Miller
Robert Miller
Karen Moeller
Eric Radzik

Jackie Riley
Kim Seyler
Ben Stewart
John Terry
Sally Westphall
Ann Willie

We could have never guessed the names I called out that morning in roll call would gain national and even international recognition for completing the monumental task of moving John Liver-eating Johnston's decayed bones from a grave in Southern California back to the Big Sky country.

Finishing up roll call, I took the remainder of the fifty minute period to explain as best I could what the next year of my Literature and American History class would look like. This was a critical moment in setting the DNA for what would be birthed in their lives over the course of the next few months. I wanted my words to be honest but challenging. Having sat where they were sitting most of my life, I knew the shoe was now on the other foot. For many years I sat and listened as teachers would lay out their courses of study and expectations of me in classes that I had been required to take. I knew the kids who were now listening to me would either leave my class-room with a sense of excitement or with thoughts that would say "same old, same old". I also knew how important it was not to fill them with unrealistic expectations, yet stir them to dream of doing things beyond the norm. As I paused, I tried to tap deep into my inner desires, asking myself the honest question, "What was it I really wanted to see happen in the lives of these students?" I knew it was more than simply teaching curriculum. I sincerely desired for their lives to be changed for the better because of the time they would invest here. I also knew they would innately sense whether what I said was sincere or simply rhetoric. Beyond everything else, my deepest hope was that they could somehow discover who they really were, and what they had been created for. As I took roll that day I could see that no two of them were alike. They each had distinct differences in their personalities and characters. I knew as their teacher the most important part of my job would be to help them grow to be the best of who they were. I knew the great trap of adolescence was a response to insecurity and inferiority that resulted in conformity; simply joining the crowd. I wanted it to be different for them. I wanted them to appreciate their uniqueness and individuality.

"Well," I started, "this class is a combination of Language Arts and American History. I've been told I can treat it as two different subjects since we have two semesters together this year. Or, we can blend it all together and spend the whole year on it as if it was one subject. That's what I'd like to do. But to be perfectly honest I'm not sure what that will look like. This will be an experiment and if we all see it as a challenge and apply ourselves to it, it could turn into a great adventure. We do have certain mandatory curriculum criteria we must fulfill, just like any class. But, we don't have to make that criterion an end in itself. Instead, it can become a launching pad for greater challenges. In other words, when you successfully take a test, proving you understand the material you are studying, that's when the learning process in this class will actually begin."

I watched their faces as I spoke and was pretty sure they weren't following me. Honestly I couldn't blame them since I didn't totally get it myself. I just knew that these kids had been taking tests their whole lives, proving they could memorize information. I wanted them to do something with the things they were learning. I knew that's where the real adventure of learning happens. Learning had to be kinetic; it had to involve action and movement of some kind. What I was saying was a paradigm shift from their previous educational experiences, so I tried to state it differently.

"Listen," I said, "we can study about American history for the sake of passing tests. You've already proven you're good at that. Or, we can learn about what has happened in the past for the sake of bringing change in our own time. That's what will make this class a creative challenge and what will give it the potential of turning into an experience none of us will ever forget."

I went on to talk about the requirements for reading and writing skills, for study and research skills, and American history in general. Then the bell rang signaling the class period had ended.

Synergy and the Power of Momentum

There are few times in a person's life when one is given the opportunity to experience the thrill and power of synergy; that momentum which sometimes happens around a human effort and occurs seemingly by accident, taking on a life of its own. I'm speaking of times where we find ourselves in the perfect place at just the right time. We are swept up with many others in a swirl of activity that excites and motivates everyone involved so that they jump in with everything they've got, bringing all they have to a table of achievement. Some of this is our doing, but much of it, from my experience, is out of our human control. It seems somehow magical. The collision of the right personalities, the right gifting, the perfect chemistry, and the supernatural timing of occurrences and events – all exploding into a ball of synergy much like a giant snowball rolling down a mountain, all the time gaining energy, getting bigger and moving faster. If we are fortunate enough we can get caught up in a snowball like that; and what a ride it can be! Human effort which often turns into striving will never create the kind of synergy I'm referring to. Some would call it a moment of fate or coincidental happenstance, but I think it's something more. I think it has to do with the divine. There is a reason for it, even though we may not see it at the moment it happens. And someday we will see it and understand.

That seventh grade class was about to experience a time just like this. Yet, on that first day of school in 1973, none of us even saw the snowball coming. We didn't even know there was one.

Synergy happens when two or more independent parts come together and create something that the individual parts could never do on their own. For example, when you purchase epoxy glue it generally comes in two separate tubes. Individually, the ingredients of each part have no intrinsic value when left alone, but when the two parts are mixed together a very powerful bonding agent is created. That's how synergy works. In my case it happened when I, as an individual teacher, came together with three other team members: Chris Wangsgard, Jane Shieh and Linda Kiel. We were assigned as part of a teaching team, all having responsibility for the same group of kids that year. Alone, none of us could have given those kids the kind of year they would experience. Together, we not only built a powerful program, but had an incredible time doing it. We were all young, full of vision and energy, and just getting started in our teaching careers. Chris had the primary role of teaching the mysteries of science; Jane explained the intricacies of math; Linda expounded on the virtues of English. And me, I dug up dead bodies. It was perfect.

In addition to the support I received from my teaching team members, we were assigned a new school principal that year. His name was Ron Huebert. Ron was younger than the previous principal and seemed to be a bit more relaxed. Years later, Linda Kiel reminded me that had it not been for the freedom Ron gave me that year, Liver-eating Johnston would probably still be rotting in his old grave. For some unknown reason,

Ron really liked me and gave me carte blanche when I proposed some of my crazy methodologies. As the story continues the truth of that will be quite evident.

Storytelling

I was given standardized textbooks to be used in teaching the general curriculum requirements. After a brief review of the textbooks, I felt they were too dry and uninspiring. I wanted more for this class. I wanted to help them learn to dream about other times in history. I wanted them to experience what I had experienced from the true-life stories I had read in college, knowing how they had changed my attitude and my way of seeing history. I wanted them to love American history, not for the sake of passing pop quizzes and regurgitating dates and events, but to understand why things happened. I desired them to feel the rhythm of those events and how one impacted the next and the next. I wanted them to understand the heart attitudes and the motivations of historical figures which caused them to do the things they did; to take the risks they took and have the willingness to suffer for greater causes than themselves. It was for this reason that I brought my own history library to class. It was a library that had grown over the past few years, made up of all the books I had read in preparation for my Master's thesis. I decided rather than making a mandate for them to read, I would take it upon myself to cultivate a hunger in them to want to read. That was why I made the decision to dedicate two days a week to telling stories about the people who had established and built the country. This was something they didn't expect, and I think it caught them off guard. The good news was that they really loved coming to class on those days, and they would always sit and intently listen.

Everyone loves storytelling. We never outgrow the love for hearing a good story. I began on the second day of school telling the tragic story of Jamestown, the first English settlement in America, whose members nearly all perished during their first bitter winters. In the days to follow I told of the first Pilgrims, and many stories that led up to the American Revolution. I told them of Washington's crossing of the Delaware in the dead of winter and the miracles that happened even in the midst of the extreme suffering of his men. I told story upon story, using historical characters and their courageous feats as the basis of my lessons. I built upon each recounting, showing how they each were woven into the fabric of the greater story of America. When I came to the events that surrounded the Louisiana Purchase in 1800, I told the story of the Lewis and Clark Expedition in great detail, drawing a huge map on the wall and locating major landmarks and significant incidents that occurred along their route.

The Lesson of the Bowie Knife

I had covered nearly two hundred years of American history, giving pop quizzes and asking students to do deeper research to extract greater detail concerning the people and events as we went. I gave them challenges like building a fire with flint and steel or making jerked meat for homework. Sometimes I would dress the part, wearing a buckskin shirt or using the large Bowie knife I still had from my old college days as a pointer when identifying things on a map or the blackboard.

At one point in my class I was about to start telling the story of the Alamo. One of the main characters in that story was Jim Bowie, who had been given credit for designing the famous Bowie knife. Bowie was to knives what Colt was to handguns. It also played an important part in American history. One day as I was speaking I mentioned to my class that I was famous for my expertise with the Bowie knife. I told them I was an artist when it came to throwing it, and was possibly even better than Jim Bowie himself. Obviously I wasn't telling the truth and everyone knew it, but it gave a little spice to my story.

One of the kids (a boy named Ron Flores, I believe) had a reputation for being vocal, and he began to goad me, demanding in a humorous way that I prove my boast. I, of course, couldn't do it for two big reasons. First, because I couldn't best Bowie even if I wanted to; and second, because throwing a large knife in a public classroom was inappropriate. This, I might add, was true even in a small country town like Lancaster in 1973. I neglected to give them the first reason, but elaborated on the second. Soon other students joined in with Ron, and even after a couple of days wouldn't let it go. That's when I secretly made a plan to vindicate myself.

Because one of my other teaching subjects was ecology in those days, I had placed a large cross section of a tree trunk on the top of a cabinet in the front of the room. The purpose of the cross section was to show the rings that aged the tree. It had been there since the first day of school. Chris Wangsgard's room and my own had an adjoining door since we were team teachers. One day during our prep period Chris kept hearing a clunking noise coming from my room and stepped through the door to see what I was up to. As he came in he saw me throwing my knife across the room at the cross section of log. "What the heck are you doing?" he asked.

"I'm trying to stick this knife in that log," I said. Then I told him about my boastful claim I had made to the kids and how they wouldn't let it go. I told him I had to make good on my Jim Bowie challenge.

I won't attempt to quote Chris's exact response, but he did say something like I was crazy and laughingly walked back out the door. He didn't want to know anymore, and definitely didn't want to be an accessory to my crime. I worked at my knife throwing skill for the better part of a week, putting small tape marks on the floor so as to know precisely where to put my toe when I made my throw. Eventually I got pretty good at hitting the mark and decided to take a chance. The next day, when the kids came to class, I casually made my claim again about being as good as Jim Bowie. As I predicted, they demanded I prove my skill just as I knew they would. Again, I reminded them that this was a public classroom and it would be inappropriate to throw such a large knife in such a place.

Further increasing the drama, I stated, "Besides, even if I did want to show you kids my skill, what could I throw it at in here?"

I had dreamt and practiced for this moment. I knew exactly what they would say. That log was too obvious. It even looked like a perfect knife-throwing target. I guess you have to have the mind of a kid to think like one, but I had called it perfectly.

They all shouted in unison, "The log; throw it at that log!"

So, without a moment's hesitation, I put my big toe on the inconspicuous tape mark on the floor, and positioned myself as I had practiced so many times before. I hurled that big knife all the way across the front of the room. It stuck perfectly dead center into the log. It was perfection at its best, and the room became a kind of silenced hush that only the awe of reverence can bring. I said nothing about it, and continued with my lesson as if it was a normal event in the day and life of Tri Robinson, history teacher.

Stories like that don't stay quiet long on any junior high school campus. It quickly circulated to every classroom, every student and every teacher by the final dismissal bell of the day. When I entered the faculty lounge that afternoon to pick up my mail, you could feel a kind of awkward tension in the air. I mean you could cut it, so to speak, with a knife.

Finally one of the older more vocal teachers, a lady named Marilyn Rogers, broke the ice. "What have you done this time, Mr. Robinson?" she asked.

"What?" I retorted, looking innocently around the lounge.

"Well," she said, "Last year you about gave me a coronary by shooting off your old Buffalo gun in the hall; I'd think you would have learned your lesson."

"It was just an object lesson," I told her. "I was teaching about Jim Bowie's fine ability to throw a knife."

Laughter started to quietly build in the room and I was grateful as it relieved the tension. I actually really loved Marilyn; she had quite a bit of mischief in her and was one lady who did help to keep me in check during my first years of teaching. I was also thankful for our new principal because of his easy-going attitude and the fact that he dismissed the event with a roll of his eyes.

I know that throwing a large knife in class would be taboo in today's culture. It wasn't the best thing to do then, but those days were very different. They were somehow much more innocent; and because of it, there was more freedom for the edgy lessons I presented over the course of the next twelve years.

CHAPTER 5

"The Committee for the Reburial of Liver-eating Johnston" is in Session

L earning the historical narrative of the development of the United States required learning the nation's geography. River systems were once the only viable means of travel so the students had to learn their names like streets or highways. They learned the names of mountain ranges and passes which were crucial for the early explorers trying to navigate their way west. They learned about the Great Plains, the vast deserts and wetlands. The students not only learned but were enthusiastic about the process. Everything was going great until a thought occurred to me. The class had only been in session for three months and I still had almost six months to go. I was starting to run out of stories. In my concern I decided the only solution was to make my stories stretch; give greater detail, use every story I could think of. And then, if all else failed, make up more.

Meeting the Man, John "Liver-eating" Johnston
I had pretty much come to the place of telling most every story

I knew when I recalled the books I had read concerning Liver-eating Johnston. I vividly remember the pivotal day I shared about Johnston's exploits as a soldier, a trapper, a logger, a military scout and a renowned Indian fighter. In the greater scheme of things Johnston's story was less important than others I could have told. When it came to his participation in the actual process of developing the West, he had little significance compared to so many others. The degree of Johnston's impact on the West had no bearing on the surprising reaction that began to grow in the classroom that day. It was far different than anything I had experienced up to that point in teaching.

As I concluded Johnston's life adventures I paused. I remembered something about his life I'd forgotten. "Do you guys know what happened to Johnston in the end?" I asked.

"What do you mean?" they questioned.

"Well," I went on, "his death was kind of anticlimactic considering how he lived and how many times he narrowly escaped getting his hair scalped off."

"How did he die?" they all asked in unison.

So I carried on my story. "Johnston retired from the harsh business of scouting, trapping and fighting in Indian conflicts, all of which so illustrated his adventurous life. I think he was probably somewhere in his late sixties by then. Anyway, he decided to settle down in the small town of Red Lodge, Montana, where he built himself a small cabin, put in a vegetable garden and was hired on as town sheriff. I suspect he would have lived out his last days there if it hadn't been for the severe case of arthritis he developed from a life of crossing frozen rivers, wading in ice cold streams to check traps and spending many nights sleeping on the wet, cold ground. By his seventies, it was said that Johnston was so stove-up that he began to rely on the charity of the residents of Red Lodge to survive. Trying to remedy his condition, he ventured south about sixty miles to Coulter's

Hell, a sulfur hot springs just outside of what is today known as Cody, Wyoming. They say he would soak his weary bones for hours on end, just lying there in the hot water until his limbs and joints would loosen up. Finally, at age seventy-two, he made a decision to take a train all the way to an old soldiers' home in the Los Angeles area here in Southern California."

"What?" They shouted. "Why would he come all the way to California to die after loving the Rocky Mountains so much?"

"Interesting, isn't it?" I stated. "Especially when he had told a friend he never wanted to leave the Montana and Wyoming country that he loved so much. It is an historical fact that he said he couldn't understand why anyone would go to a foreign country like California where everyone speaks a different language."

"What do you mean?" they asked. "What different language?"

"Well," I said, "In Johnston's earlier days, California had been a part of Mexico and I think he didn't realize how civilized it had become by the year 1900. Due to his war experience, he knew he could get free medical help through his veteran's rights. So, he took the train to California and arrived on January 1st, 1900; it was the first day of the new millennium. He died just two days later and was buried in a soldier's uniform in the Sawtelle Veteran Cemetery, located near UCLA by the San Diego Freeway."

It was a sad ending to a story about a man with such a rich history and legacy. There was no question about that. But the reaction of my students that day was so profound that it completely caught me off guard.

"What?" they cried in unison. "That can't be! That's just wrong!" With that, they became outraged at the thought of Liver-eating Johnston, their famous mountain man, being buried in the middle of a hectic, smog-filled city, literally a hundred yards from the San Diego Freeway. Some even stood up in protest.

"Hold on!" I yelled above their angry outburst. "Settle down a minute. All that happened nearly seventy-five years ago. It's a done deal."

Their reaction was something I couldn't have anticipated. I agreed with them, but I hadn't personally viewed his burial site as an outright injustice the way they did. The release bell rang and all twenty-four students sulked out of the classroom leaving me to wonder. In the three months I'd been teaching them, this was the first time I'd experienced that kind of passion about anything from the students.

Nancy's Big Idea

Later that evening I got back to our little ranch and found Nancy standing over the kitchen woodstove cooking dinner. The first thing I told her was about how the class had reacted to Johnston's death and place of burial.

I leaned over the counter and stated, "You wouldn't believe what happened today."

"What's that?" she answered as she continued preparing dinner.

"Well," I said, "my kids wanted to revolt because of a story I told them about that old mountain man, Liver-eating Johnston."

"Oh really," she responded. "Why was that?"

So I told her the whole story, reminding her of where Johnston had been laid to rest. Then, I remember so clearly how she casually looked up from what she was doing and made a very short but life-changing comment.

She simply stated, "If they don't like it, tell them to move him."

"Move him?" I questioned. "How could they move him?"

"Well," she said, "even if they can't move him they could learn a lot from trying. Besides, I think they could do it with you as their teacher."

With that brief statement swirling in my brain, I spent the remainder of the evening pondering what I would say to my class the next day. Because one of my objectives for the fall was teaching a unit on formal letter writing, I concluded that I could at least use this new development to motivate them to write to historical societies, governors and other significant people of Montana, Wyoming and Idaho. They could petition for permission and support to rebury a man who had been underground for seventy five years. I had absolutely no idea what would be involved in moving a gravesite, especially the grave of an American veteran. I was undaunted as I began to consider my seventh grade students and how to provide them an incentive for learning to write a few formal letters.

If I was going to have them write these letters I figured they would need a formal letterhead. That formal letterhead would require a title for the organization sending such letters, so as to appear official and all. With that in mind, I wrote on a piece of notebook paper that night what I would take to the printer the next day. It would be a letterhead written in western script that said:

The Committee for the Reburial of Liver-eating Johnston
Park View School, 808 West Avenue J
Lancaster, California 93534

The next day the kids entered the classroom like any other day. Who knew that this day would mark the beginning of a series of amazing and unexpected events? I had no idea that what was about to happen would someday be worthy of a memoir or even an article in an obscure educator's journal.

Today, as I attempt to accurately record all the events that led up to the reburial of Liver-eating Johnston, I wish I'd had the forethought to chronicle it all from that seemingly normal day to the ending of the school year. There was no way of knowing at that time what would happen eventually. In fact, for a while it looked quite hopeless.

The Big Sell

The tardy bell rang and all twenty-four kids were sitting in their seats. I paused before the class and asked, "By any chance, do you remember what I told you the first day of school?"

They sort of squirmed in their seats; of course they didn't. So I tried as best I could to recount the basics of my opening lecture again that day, summarizing how real learning begins after the tests and pop quizzes were taken.

"Do you guys remember me saying I wasn't sure what this class would end up looking like, and that it would be an experiment of sorts? I told you that we would be taking the mandatory curriculum and turning it into a real life history project. I also said that the curriculum would only serve as a launching pad for the real learning adventure. I didn't want us to just study American History in order to take a test, but to respond to it and use our knowledge for the sake of changing things now, in the time we live."

I could tell they were intently listening, wondering where my little lecture was going to end up. I had their attention so I seized the moment and went on. "I also told you that if we decided to go the extra mile together, it would give our class the potential of turning this into an experience none of us would ever forget. Do you guys remember any of that?" I asked.

A few heads started to nod as they began to see where this oration was headed.

"Okay then," I said, trying to drive my point home. "Here, then, is my proposal. I think if you guys are so upset about the burial site of Liver-eating Johnston being here in California, then you should do something about it. Too many people complain about things they see as being wrong without ever trying to make them right. "

"How could we do that?" they came back. "What are we supposed to do, go to the cemetery and dig him up?" they asked.

I couldn't help but laugh at their initial reaction and responded, "Yep, something like that. But, first you need to have the proper authority and permission, which we might just get by writing letters to the right people."

Then, with all eyes fixed expectantly on me, I made a statement that was received by them as a promise. I echoed the words Nancy had spoken the night before, "I think you guys can do it!"

At that, I lowered my voice an octave or two and said in the most official sounding way I could, "From this day forth this class will no longer be referred to as the seventh grade Literature and American History class, but instead will forever be called, 'The Committee for the Reburial of Liver-eating Johnston'!"

For a second the class went quiet as my words rattled around inside their teenage brains. It reminded me of the pressure that builds deep inside a volcano right before the eruption. Then it came, first with a few, then with the mass.

"Hurray!" they yelled; "Hurray for The Committee for the Reburial of Liver-eating Johnston!"

Then, they used a word that was only reserved for the most amazing things imaginable during those days of the early 1970's. And, they used it in reference to me.

"Mr. Robinson is GROOVY!" someone shouted, and then others echoed the compliment few teachers would ever receive; "Yeah!" they joined in, "Mr. Robinson is a groovy teacher!"

I was in big trouble. I had arrived at the pinnacle of teacher popularity; and it was a place I never imagined I'd be. I knew other teachers were groovy. I knew, for example, that Linda Kiel was considered totally groovy. She was born groovy. Not me. Not a dyslexic kid who struggled to even read a book.

I knew I'd really done it now. I had actually convinced them they could get a dead man's grave moved if they worked hard enough. I had sold them on the idea that they could make a difference in the world, even if they were only seventh graders. In my attempt to get them to learn to write a few letters I had convinced them that Johnston's body could actually be moved. The reality hit, and it hit me hard. I was at the top of the pinnacle; and from where I was standing there was only one place to go: down! And my descent might come sooner rather than later.

The Project Begins

I had worked very late the night before, coming up with as many names as I could for potential recipients of my students' letters. I made a list of historical societies, government agencies and officials; those I felt might show interest or could somehow help out in this farfetched venture. I even included CEOs of large corporations I knew were based in the Big Sky states. My list only included the three Big Sky states; even though Johnston wandered anywhere he pleased in his time without concern for borders. Montana and Wyoming, for example, were just names within survey lines and had no impact on the free spirits of mountain men or Indians. I say this now because state lines would become a major issue before the story I'm recounting would have its happy ending.

Naturally, the first place they wrote to was the chamber of commerce and historical society of Red Lodge, Montana. This was obvious as it was the last known residence of the Liver-eater. We figured if any group of people would be enthusiastic about moving Johnston's grave, it would definitely be them.

Every student participated, writing letter after letter that was both sincere and compelling about their mission. Day after day they received no response at all. Or if they did, it was just a polite form letter that felt much like a pat on the head to the students.

Because the committee needed a chairman, the class held an election that day and selected fellow classmate, Eric Radzik. He seemed to be one of the most enthusiastic in the bunch and embraced his new job seriously. Eric and his friend, Ben Stewart, took it upon themselves to go straight to the Governor of Montana with their request. Their letter was clearly written from the standpoint of a junior high school student; it was right to the point.

Dear Governor:

We are a committee who is combined to change the burial site of a famous historical figure.

I'd like to tell you about a man who once roamed your country in the mountain man era. His name is Liver-Eating Johnston. He lived in the Big Sky country for many years and became very strong and powerful. He was a loner for many years when he finally got married to an Indian Squaw. They roamed the mountain lands together for many years when they finally settled down and built a house. That winter Johnston went trapping and left his wife home. He was gone awhile when he got a terrible feeling. He jumped on his horse and rode home as fast as he could, only to find his wife and unborn son dead in the ruins of a burned, smoldering house.

He scouted around and found that Crow Indians had killed his wife and son. He made a vow that he would kill many Crow warriors and eat their livers. It was this deed that made him a famous person. In his old age he got sick and was sent to the V.A. hospital in Los Angeles, 100 yards from the San Diego Freeway.

We would like Liver-Eating Johnston reburied in Red Lodge, Montana, and his last residence. Your support would be greatly appreciated.

If you wish to support us in this venture, please contact us with some constructive ideas.

Sincerely,

Eric Radzik & Ben Stewart

The Committee for the Reburial

of Liver-Eating Johnston

In retrospect, reading their letter through the eyes of a state governor, it does seem a bit farfetched to believe he would help a bunch of adolescent kids dig up and rebury a man who allegedly ate the livers of Indians. The governor did respond, however, saying something about Montana having many Indian constituents from several tribes. Because of this, he did not believe it advantageous to support an effort to memorialize a man who not only killed Indians, but cannibalized them. Looking back on it now, I guess I couldn't blame him for his response. At the time, though, it was very defeating to our committee.

In actuality, Johnston never really did eat the liver of an Indian. His nickname came from an event that gave him not only the name but also a reputation he could not shake the rest of his life. Historians say that he was given the name when he fought a number of Sioux Indian braves. After stabbing and mortally wounding a young brave with a large knife, a piece of the Indian's liver came out. Johnston raised the knife, holding the liver out to his comrades, he asked them if they wanted a bite. He later told a friend that he had rubbed some of the liver in his beard to make his partners think he'd really eaten it. But according to Johnston, he really never did. From that point on the infamous name, "Liver-eater", stuck. It might be understandable that the Governor of Montana wasn't too motivated to accept the students' proposal, but it would come back to haunt him later.

A First Glimmer of Hope

Days turned into weeks without a single encouraging response. The momentum, fueled by each letter the students had written, began to slowly dissipate. Things were looking a little grim when, a few weeks later, a letter appeared in my faculty mail box. It was addressed to the students of Park View School and the Committee for the Reburial of Liver-eating Johnston. The letter was from my old friend, Bob Edgar, in Cody, Wyoming. It was a very welcomed first gleam of hope. Bob's response was actually an unexpected surprise. First, I had forgotten that I added his name to the list of recipients. And second, I couldn't remember editing any letter written in my class that was addressed to him. Bob was a very significant resource to me during my work on my Master's project for the College of Idaho several years before.

The next morning after everyone was seated, I asked the question, "Did anyone here write a letter to a guy named Bob Edgar in Cody, Wyoming?" My eyes scanned the room.

Finally a small kid towards the back of the room named Russ Gilliam tentatively raised his hand. He said, "I think I did, Mr. Robinson."

"When did you write it?" I asked. Then I added, "I don't recall correcting any letter written to Cody during class time."

"I wrote it from home," Russ said. "I didn't think you'd mind. My mom mailed it for me."

It turned out that Russ had written two weeks before, when

our excitement about the project was still mounting. He had taken it upon himself to make some extra contacts, and Bob had been one of them. It turned out it was a miracle to even get a response because Bob later told me the letter was addressed to *Bos Escar from Cozy, Wyoming.* The most amazing part was that Bob took it seriously enough to respond. In his reply he wrote that if our seventh grade committee could get permission to move Johnston's body, he would pay for everything if we were willing to inter him in Old Trail Town.

That day Russ Gilliam was the class hero. If it hadn't been for his initiative to go above and beyond, to this day Liver-eating Johnston would still be resting under a cloud of freeway smog. Bob's letter to the committee broke the streak of defeat and disappointment. It was the first sign of hope and did much to lift our spirits. But, we still needed some major miracles to get permission for our crazy venture. Though we had no way of knowing it at the time, those miracles would come in some amazing and surprising ways over the course of the weeks that followed.

CHAPTER 6

Transitional Events

Enter Robert Redford as "Jeremiah Johnson"

Over the course of the next several months some events happened that could only be called miracles. They were things that couldn't have been orchestrated in any way to make the final outcome of the reburial project come to pass. One was a movie that finally made its way to Lancaster, California. The Warner Bros. production, *Jeremiah Johnson*, starred Robert Redford and was first released in December of 1972 at the Cannes Film Festival. It was filmed in Utah, Redford's home state, but premiered in Boise, Idaho. Somehow it didn't make it to Lancaster until November of the following year. And until then, we didn't even know the theme of the movie. I remember being anxious for it to be released in our local theaters, not because I knew it was the story of Liver-eating Johnston, but because I both appreciated Redford's acting and loved western movies in general. *Butch Cassidy and the Sundance Kid*, a movie Redford starred in with Paul Newman, had been a favorite of mine. In fact, it was the first movie I took Nancy to see when we started dating in 1969. I distinctly remember that because I got her back to her dorm room after curfew and she had to sneak in through a laundry room window to avoid getting caught. As she went through the opening she started to fall and grabbed the Venetian blinds nearly ripping them off the brackets that held them. The resulting commotion could have wakened the dead, even at 1:00 a.m. in the morning. It was such a memorable night that we later used the movie's theme song, *Raindrops Keep Fallin' on My Head,* in our wedding.

One morning as I unlocked the classroom door, my student aide, Paul Kinoyo, excitedly ran up to me. Paul was a student in my class the previous year and was such a great kid that I had asked him to be my aide. Paul was ecstatic as he approached and was speaking so fast I wasn't able to understand a word he said. I couldn't help but laugh as I told him to slow down, take a breath and start over. Paul was of Japanese descent; he was small in stature but big on enthusiasm. That enthusiasm was contagious. He was the kind of kid every teacher enjoyed having around.

On that day Paul was more enthusiastic than ever; in fact, he was totally out of control. Not even listening to my admonition to calm down a bit, he simply blurted out, "Have you seen the movie *Jeremiah Johnson?*"

"No, I haven't," I said; "but I've really been looking forward to it."

He quickly replied without hesitation, "Did you know it's about our mountain man, Liver-eating Johnston?"

"Why, no," I responded as the reality of his statement began to sink in. "You've got to be kidding!"

"It's true!" he stated excitedly. "It's all about him, and it's really good. It tells the whole story you told us."

It really was a miracle, I thought, to have a movie about this obscure historical character come out at the perfect time. Until then, we had to explain to everyone who Johnston was before we could even communicate our plan to move his grave.

With the movie and storyline gaining in appreciation, Johnston was rapidly becoming an internationally known personality. This made our job much easier. In fact, it served as a major shot in the arm for our committee's quest.

When the class met that morning, obviously the first thing we did was write a letter to Robert Redford. Of course with his growing fame at the time, it was no wonder we didn't receive a response. At least not for a while, anyway.

Richard Keelor: Personal Ambassador to Washington D.C.
At the time my dad was principal of Beverly Hills High School. He held the most prestigious position that public education in America could offer in that day. Beverly Hills had its own school district, and because the city had so much money, much of it was poured into the education system. The high school had a gymnasium floor that rolled back with the touch of a lever, exposing an Olympic-sized swimming pool hidden underneath. Another hydraulic control raised both high and low diving boards. The school had its own planetarium as well as a performing arts program that was next to none. The staff was compiled of some of the best educators around, which explains why Dr. Richard Keelor, the varsity football coach, was such an amazing guy. Dick, as we called him, received a request that year from the United States Government to fill the position as head of the President's Council for Physical Fitness. His acceptance required him to move to Washington D.C. Everyone at Beverly Hills High was sad about the loss of Dick as part of the faculty. He did, however, come back often to Southern California on business. And when he did, he made a point to stop in at the school for a visit.

On one such visit he actually came up to our ranch to spend time with my dad who was staying with Nancy and me for the weekend. Dick was a good friend of ours as well so we invited him to stay for the night. He happily accepted the invitation and we settled in for the evening. As we ate dinner, he asked how my new teaching assignment was going. This quickly led to a conversation whereby I told him about The Committee for the Reburial of Liver-eating Johnston and all we had accomplished so far that year.

I remember Dick asking, "So, now that your kids have the financial support to move Johnston through your friend in Cody, what else do they need?"

"Permission," I stated. "We need permission."

With that I expounded on the facts we had thus far learned. In order for a body to be disinterred, you had to have permission from the next of kin. As yet, we had been unable to find anyone who wanted to claim Johnston as family. Dick asked if there were any other alternatives. I told him we would need official written permission from the Veteran's Administration in Washington D.C. I added that this seemed highly unlikely for a bunch of seventh graders to obtain.

"Well," said Dick; "That's one place I think I can help you."

"How's that?" I asked, not sure I believed what I was hearing.

Dick went on to say that the head of the Veteran's Administration, Rufus Wilson, had his office just down the hall from his own. They had become close friends and often went to lunch together.

"Oh yeah," said Dick. "Rufus and I are good friends, and I know he'll be glad to help you out. If not," he went on, "I'll put him in a good old fashion Liver-eating Johnston headlock until he does."

That was to become our second miracle that month. No one could have predicted a chance meeting with Dick Keelor would occur at such a perfect time.

Within a couple weeks, my class received a letter from Rufus Wilson himself. As I read the formal letter, written on very official government stationary, the class was intently listening to every word Mr. Wilson had written. It stated that he would be going through a congressional process that would name our class as the official next of kin of John Johnston. This would allow us to go ahead with the disinterment. He said that he would contact his associate, Theodore Nick, who was head of the V.A. cemetery in Los Angeles. Mr. Wilson would inform him of this key decision on the next of kin. Now we not only had the funds for the project, but also official government permission to make our move. This would lead to the awakening of the press; up to this point a sleeping giant regarding our endeavors.

Chuck Johnston: A Distant Relative

The first publicity started in our own home town of Lancaster. The Valley Press, our local paper, began printing articles about the committee's intentions, some of which appeared on the front page. Eventually, the story actually hit the Associated Press. Immediately papers such as the L.A. Times started picking up the story and sending reporters to visit our class. Articles were printed about our progress in the quest thus far. As one can only imagine, this propelled our synergy snowball forward, causing a plethora of new events to transpire. Not long after the L.A. Times article was published, we received a phone call from a man in Corona, California. His name was Chuck Johnston and he claimed that John Johnston was his great uncle.

Chuck was a really likeable guy. A construction worker by trade, he told us that while he was growing up his father took him once a year on Veterans Day to visit Johnston's gravesite. Chuck said he never thought of his Uncle John as being famous, he just knew he had been an Indian fighter and trapper somewhere in the northern part of the country. He had read the article about us looking for Johnston's next of kin and announced he was ready and willing to help if he could. At first we weren't sure what to think about Chuck's claim. This all happened long before forensic science performed everyday DNA testing. Even if that testing was available, we would still need a sample of Johnston's bones to confirm the match. That would require digging him up, and we couldn't dig him up without the permission of next of kin. It all came back to the same predicament; we needed that permission, whether from a committee of students named as official next of kin, or from a distant relative of Johnston's. No matter the situation, Chuck became another incredible ingredient in the story. The moment we saw him in person, we knew there was no question he was related to our mountain man. He possessed an amazing resemblance to his great uncle. We knew this because of the historical photos we had studied of Johnston as a younger man. Also, Chuck's carefree spirit and easy-going mannerism gave him away as well. We could easily envision Chuck Johnston following in his famous uncle's footsteps, leaving civilization and living a life of rugged solitude.

Roy Neil Drops By from NBC

The next remarkable event came about in the form of another phone call. This time from a man named Roy Neil. He was a well-known news correspondent for NBC, most famous for being the lead commentator on all the NASA moon shots. He covered the very first lunar landing as well as many of the first orbits. We were elated when Roy asked to bring a film crew to our classroom to do personal interviews with our class. He became not only an inspiration to the class but a true comrade in our venture. For the interview, Roy told us he would use footage filmed in Lancaster with additional footage they would shoot during the reburial ceremony in Cody. He said he would fly to Wyoming and personally meet us there. In the end, his involvement saved the entire project from collapsing during a last minute crisis.

A Surprising Call from Redford

In May of that year a reporter from the L.A. Times came to do some personal interviews with the students. In the context of the interview he asked if Robert Redford had answered our correspondence. We told him Redford hadn't, but that it didn't really surprise us too much.

The following week the L.A. Times posted an article telling the story of our quest, stating that a group of seventh graders were trying to right an injustice to an American legend. It also said that Robert Redford had not responded to their cry for help. The article had Redford's picture as Jeremiah Johnson alongside it, naturally drawing extra attention to the piece. A week later another article appeared. This time it was on the front page of the L.A. Times, with the headline, "*Redford is Red-faced over lost letter.*" The article claimed Redford had been livid because somebody lost or misplaced a thank-you letter he'd written to a class of seventh graders at Park View Junior High School in Lancaster. The story alleged that Redford said if the reburial was actually going to happen, he might consider sneaking up to the interment ceremony to join the kids there. That put a whole new level of excitement into the atmosphere of our class, specifically with my twelve-year-old girls who were gaining awareness of an entirely new application for American History. The growing snowball began to gain even more speed.

Chicken Soup for the Teenage Soul

A few days later, after the L.A. Times article concerning Redford's so-called response to our plight, there was yet another astounding occurrence. I was called to the school office to take a phone call. This was highly unusual, considering the fact that I would have to leave the room for a time. Usually a message would be taken unless it was an extreme emergency. I recall feeling a little anxious because of the peculiarity of the situation.

This particular part of the story is best told by one of my students who was there that day. His name is Kif Anderson, and he later recalled the event in a chapter he had published in the book, *Chicken Soup for the Teenage Soul.* He recorded, "Mr. Robinson came back with a glow on his face like we had never seen before and said, "Guess who that was on the phone!" Kip wrote on; "Robert Redford had called and said he received hundreds of letters every day and that ours somehow had never reached him, but he was very interested in helping us achieve our goal. Suddenly our team was not only getting bigger, it was getting more influential and powerful."

From then on, nearly every day we received phone calls important enough that I wanted the students to be part of them. Because we didn't have a phone in our classroom, the only place we could take the call was in the main office. When one came into the office, they would call us over the classroom intercom system. If I felt it was pertinent, I would tell the class to quietly walk to the main office so as not to upset any teachers or classes along the way. Years later, Linda Kiel told me that every time that happened it sounded like a herd of wild horses stampeding down the hall. I guess we couldn't contain the excitement we felt. The principal, Ron Huebert, was amazing through it all. He often allowed the students to crowd into his private office with the phone on speaker so everyone could hear the conversation. This also helped in keeping us from disrupting the main office secretaries too much.

Western Airlines: "The Only Way to Fly"
One of the phone calls the class received was from a major airline. In those days Western Airlines was one of the top carriers in the U.S. They often advertised on television, famous for their tagline, *"The only way to fly."* They called to offer to fly the students free of charge from Los Angeles International Airport (LAX) to West Yellowstone Park. Our destination, Cody, was

just east of Yellowstone and a little over a hundred miles. They said they wanted the students to experience a little of the country Johnston had roamed before the reinterment ceremony in Cody. The students still had to come up with enough funds for the return flight to California, hotel rooms in Cody, some meals and transportation from West Yellowstone to the reburial site at Old Trail Town. That was too much for many of them; therefore only about half the class was able to make the trip. It was decided that those who wouldn't be going to Wyoming would represent the class at the disinterment in Los Angeles. That way everyone could participate in the unforgettable experience on some level.

As invitations for the reburial ceremony were sent out, preparations were being made for thousands of people to show up in Cody in early June. It actually began to look as if our dream would come to pass. That is, until some unexpected bad news arrived only hours before Johnston's appointed time of disinterment in Los Angeles. In those final hours, everything turned very dark.

CHAPTER 7

The Twelfth Hour

Everything started happening really fast during the last days of May and the first week of June. School was almost finished for another year, and yet more transpired in those last two weeks than almost any other time during the year. Until then our progress to complete our goal of moving Johnston had been a month-to-month struggle. Suddenly, it took on a life of its own, changing day-to-day and sometimes hour-by-hour. Our hard fought battle to see our quest to completion seemed close to victory.

**Teaching to the Uniqueness of Every Student:
A Gift to Cherish**

Besides our efforts as The Committee for the Reburial of Liver-eating Johnston, we did lots of other learning assignments as a class. Much of the work we did together built lasting and deep relationships between us. In those days I would often take students home to our ranch for a night or a weekend to do additional projects. Nancy would teach the girls historical skills like how use a treadle sewing machine, how to cook on a wood-burning cook stove, the art of Dutch oven cooking over an open fire, and how to preserve food. I would teach on lost skills such as how to use a blacksmith's hand-crank forge. I also let students help me shoe a horse or use a team of horses to pull a wagon or farming implement. I even taught them how to load and shoot a vintage black powder rifle. Times were very different in those days; I'd be the first to admit that. Sometimes I think back on the often unconventional methods I used in teaching my students. Even I'm surprised as I consider some of the potentially dangerous things I would allow them to do without undo concern for legal ramifications.

Sadly, I realize in today's world where educators continually feel threatened by litigation, the types of activities I did in those days wouldn't be allowed in any educational curriculum. Once I actually took a history class on a three-day wagon train trip around our valley. Some students rode their own horses, while others harnessed and drove wagons. We had two very near mishaps on that trip which we later all laughed about, making it a very memorable learning experience. Reflecting on all we did then, I wonder if we have allowed our changing culture to rob kids of the rich experiential learning that can only happen when we step out of the norm and brave the creative chasm to a road less traveled.

Looking back at all we were allowed to do as educators in those days, I can't help but feel a little sorrow. We took for granted the freedom we had as teachers in the 1970's; we didn't realize then how quickly things were going to change. The fear of liability and lawsuits has slowly deprived teachers of the desire to step out of the box and freely dream of kinetic, creative ways to energize and teach kids. In our day, we thought nothing of taking students off campus; even in my case to my home for a project. This was all done without fear of some sort of repercussion. The culture in general was far more innocent in those days. Having been out of public education for many years, I'm probably not the best resource on all of this. It does appear, from my perspective, that the education system is slowly entering a state of paralysis with much emphasis on tools like standardized testing. I'm not sure how it works today, but it would have forced a teacher like me to spend much valuable time teaching to tests rather than individualizing my program based on the uniqueness of the kids in my class. I do understand the concept "no child left behind"; perhaps more than most due to my own learning struggles. And, I thank God for a man like Mr. Hanson, who years ago felt that concern for me. At the same time, after years of teaching, I realize every student in every classroom in America is unique; and because of that, there is not "one method of teaching" that fits all. Educators must have the freedom to create and consider who they are teaching to in the process.

From my experiences in life, I have found that authentic relationships emerge as people accomplish significant things together. Relationships that fail to share common goals or vision often don't have any lasting impact. It's been over forty years since that amazing group of kids was together as seventh graders. Even now I would venture to say that not one of them has forgotten they were a part of such an unorthodox experience as moving a dead man's gravesite. Conflict and struggle are often the tools that etch a life event indelibly on the human mind. When people come together to fight for victory over a crisis or unsurmountable obstacle, they never forget it. Especially when all their efforts pay off in the end. In the weeks preceding Johnston's scheduled reburial there was an abundance of conflict.

Twelfth Hour Conflict

Our crisis began with a phone call that came from Rufus Wilson's office in Washington D.C. Rufus himself didn't make the call; it was someone else on his staff who was assigned as the bearer of some very bad news.

I was called to the office on Monday afternoon, May 26th. The call came just as the final dismissal bell was ringing. Though I don't remember the name of the person I spoke with, their message is one I'll never forget. It was quick and to the point, delivered in a very matter-of-fact tone.

"Mr. Robinson, I have been asked to inform you that the disinterment scheduled for one o'clock tomorrow afternoon has been cancelled. I have also been asked to tell you not to take your students to the V.A. cemetery as planned; and for your class not to pursue activities involving the reburial of Mr. Johnston until you receive further notice from our office."

I was shocked. Everything had been going according to plan. It had been like clockwork, and my students were in a state of ecstatic anticipation. At that very moment many of them were on their way home, thinking about personally witnessing the disinterment the following day.

It took me a second to gather my thoughts before responding to the person on the other end of the line. I was aware that he was just about to hang up when I jumped in asking, "What's this about; what happened?"

"I am not at liberty to say," he replied. "I have only been authorized to tell you that it has been called off."

"Wait a minute!" I shot back. "You can't just say that without some explanation!"

His reply was even shorter than before. He simply said, "Goodbye."

That was it. The entire call was over in a matter of a minute or two, and it left me reeling.

I didn't know what to do. I ran into Ron Huebert's office almost in tears. I told him what had happened and he, too, was in a total state of shock. Over the past month the reburial had been announced in papers all across the nation, and even in other parts of the world. In just twelve short days, people would be traveling to Cody from all over the country to witness the event.

Several of the girls in our class had collected news clippings and posted them on our classroom bulletin board. With so much press coverage, we were starting to run out of space. Even family and friends from other states sent the students clippings from their local papers. These were added to the collection. It truly felt to me as if the eyes of the whole world were upon us; and the weight of the world was on my shoulders. The weight, at that moment, was more than I could bear. Without knowing what else to do, I did what I often did. I called my dad at his office in Beverly Hills to share my burden and ask his advice.

Thankfully, Dad was in his office at the time and immediately took my call. It was unusual to hear from me at that time of the day so he must have suspected a problem.

"What's up, Tri?" he asked with some hesitancy.

"Dad," I said dejectedly. "I have a real problem."

"What is it?" he responded with real concern in his voice.

I told him about the phone call and all of the preparations already in motion. I also said that I felt responsible for the whole mess.

Then I asked with desperation in my voice, "What do you think I should do?"

He asked me some more questions and then paused. "Well…" he said; "Here's what I think I would do."

Often he would frame things like that, not wanting me to think he was telling me what he thought I should do. In that way I could simply receive it as counsel. At that moment, I was too desperate to care. I really did want to know what he thought I should do.

Then he went on, "I think I'd give Roy Neil, your new friend over at NBC, a call. I'd do it right now before he goes home for the day."

That was something I hadn't thought of and it gave me hope.

He continued, "First of all you need to know what's really going on. And if anyone can find out, it's Roy Neil. I would bet there has been some political pressure put on the V.A. and they probably got cold feet. Also, Roy has a personally vested interest in the project, having sent a news team to both Lancaster and Cody. He will certainly be motivated to see your project succeed."

"Anyway," he went on. "That's what I'd do. Let me know what you find out. Meanwhile, I'll be working on things from my office."

As I write this all down (in 2014), my dad is now ninety-five years old. I can still remember what a comfort it was that afternoon to know that I had him working on my team.

Roy Neil and NBC News to the Rescue

As soon as I hung up from the call with Dad, I immediately dialed the number Roy Neil had given me. He had told me if we needed any help, not to hesitate giving him a call. I did so now without hesitation. He answered the phone right away. Another miracle in this whole story is that I actually reached him on the first ring. I instantly unloaded about everything that had happened as fast as I could.

"Hum-m-m…" said Roy. "Sounds like a fly in the ointment . . . probably political."

"That's exactly what my Dad said!" I told him. "What should I do?"

Roy was a very thoughtful man. Not wanting to say too much out of turn, he simply told me to hang on. "I'll tell you what," he said, "why don't you stick by your phone there at school and let me call you back in a few minutes. I want to think about this and talk to a few of my colleagues. I'll call you back in ten minutes, and let you know what we come up with."

"Okay," I said. "And thank you so much, Roy." With that I hung up the phone.

The next ten minutes were some of the longest of my life. I just sat there with my head in my hands, thinking about what the failure of this year-long venture would mean. How it would affect the twenty-four students who had come to believe in not only me but the possibility of making a difference. I was devastated.

Ron and the rest of the administrative staff waited with me. I realized then, this had become much more than a class project. It had captured the heart of the entire school district, and they were now feeling ownership of the Johnston project as well. Much later I found out our district's superintendent, Dr. Bruce Newlin, had taken the initiative to personally contact our U.S. Congressmen, Bill Ketchum and John Rousse, to investigate the delay. I began to realize how many amazing people had come to our rescue.

The phone rang. Sure enough Roy Neil was on the other end. "Okay," he said without any introduction. "Here's what we're going to do."

Roy spoke these few words with confidence and assurance. Something I desperately needed right then. I knew from his first statement that he had some sort of a plan. This meant I wasn't in a corner. There would be other options; other moves could be made.

Roy went on, "First of all, your dad and I were right when we thought there must be political pressure. There is, and here's what happened. As you probably know, nobody had originally taken your students seriously. I mean, no one actually thought they could pull this off. Then, you got Redford involved and more publicity than even a moon shot. Everyone was elated to see a bunch of seventh grade kids do something so amazing, simply by writing letters and having some fortitude. That was an inspiration. When the people in Red Lodge, Montana realized this thing was actually going to happen, they got envious and contacted their congressman, John Melchar. He called your Mr. Rufus Wilson in D.C. and questioned his right to give a bunch of kids in Lancaster the authority to do such a thing. He also contacted the VFW (Veterans of Foreign Wars) in D.C. and asked them to join him in intervening."

Holy smokes, I thought. What a mess! Who would have believed that two dozen kids could have stirred up such a ruckus?

Roy then went on with humor in his voice. "So," he said. "Here's the plan. I'm going to send a crew to film and interview your class first thing in the morning. I want you to call your friend, Bob Edgar, in Cody. Tell him to get out there tonight and dig a big hole in the location he plans to bury Johnston. Tell him to expect a crew to come up and film him, showing all the preparations that have been made at Old Trail Town. When that's done I'll be calling our friend, Rufus Wilson, to tell him if he doesn't make a good decision by sundown on behalf of your kids, he's going to experience the worst publicity the V.A.'s ever had. I'm more than sure that should fix the problem."

Wow, I thought! I had no idea until that moment just how powerful the media could be when it came to getting things done. I wasn't quite sure what to think about it; if it was a good thing or bad thing. At that moment, in that circumstance, I felt certain it was a good thing. At least it was for The Committee on the Reburial of Liver-eating Johnston.

As instructed, I made the phone call to Bob and he got going on the digging. Then, I headed home and told Nancy all that had transpired. As I recall I had a fairly sleepless night.

The next morning Rufus Wilson called the school at exactly nine o'clock. His voice sounded extremely stressed. I think he must have had a sleepless night as well. All I really remember about the conversation was him saying, "Get your kids down to the cemetery this morning as soon as possible. Johnston's body will be disinterred and transported to LAX this morning. If he isn't, his reburial will never happen."

In addition to his message of urgency, he also told me not to take more than a few students with me to the disinterment due to his fear of having it look like a spectacle. He was deathly afraid of getting any more bad press. I was saddened by his instructions, knowing the disappointment it would bring to the students who couldn't attend. With great regret I told him I would follow his directions, said a final thank you, and then walked back to my class with the news.

Accusations of Being "Grave Robbers"

One of the students entered the classroom with a copy of that morning's L.A. Times. She opened the paper to an article entitled, "*Grave Robbers!" charges VFW on Jeremiah Johnson Reburial Plans.* The article stated that the Veterans of Foreign Wars was accusing our class, Rufus Wilson, and the Veterans Administration Office in Washington, D.C. of being grave robbers. It said, "With precedents such as this no veteran remains safe in his grave."

Later, another article was posted as a rebuttal to the VFW accusation. In it, Rufus Wilson was quoted as saying he had investigated the project thoroughly and that the seventh graders "were publically spirited citizens carrying out Johnston's last wish to be buried in mountain country." He went on to state, "We had ample legal authority to do what we were doing." In addition to that, he informed the media that our students had contacted all three of the Big Sky states, but only Wyoming showed any support and was enthusiastic about their efforts.

For the next few days news stories surrounding the situation started to fly. One memorable article came from the local paper in Red Lodge, Montana. I'm not sure the article was meant for eyes outside of their own area, as it acknowledged the fact that the motive for getting Johnston's body to Red Lodge was to boost tourism in their community. Because that wasn't the heart of our intent for having Johnston moved, it helped to confirm we made the right decision in selecting Cody as the final resting place for his bones. This was right since so much of Johnston's history in Big Sky territory had taken place there.

While on a phone call with Bob Edgar, he mentioned he'd been receiving menacing phone calls and letters which made threatening accusations against him personally. Things really started to heat up, and I should have been worried for Bob. And I would have been worried, except for the fact that this was the same guy who shot a charging bear with only a handgun. I figured he could take care of whatever hostility that came his way.

Meanwhile, Rufus Wilson hoped that his final decision would settle once and for all the squabble between the citizens of Red Lodge and Cody. Unfortunately, as the story continued to unfold, it didn't.

CHAPTER 8

Digging Up Johnston

A Delegation of Five for Disinterment

I'm not sure why Pat McIver, Jackie Riley and Sally West-phal were the three students chosen to represent the class at Johnston's disinterment, but I do remember what great kids they were. The day took a few unexpected turns and they were not only respectful but flexible enough to flow with the changes we experienced. Everything had happened fast as a result of Rufus Wilson's phone call and I didn't have a chance to reorganize the new plans for our trip down to the cemetery. In those days I drove a 1951 Dodge truck to commute to and from the Ranch. This was not an adequate vehicle to transport students on the Los Angeles Freeway, so the school district came to my aid by sending Katie Corbett to the rescue. Katie's official title was "School Community Liaison Representative" and she had been our committee's advocate from the beginning, helping us get the word out about our project. She showed up driving a huge boat of a car. After inviting our small delegation to jump in, we headed for Sawtelle Veteran's Cemetery on that Tuesday morning, May 27th.

It took two very long hours to get there. The anticipation was so great between the three kids in the backseat you could have cut it with a knife (not a Bowie knife, of course.) Obviously none of us had ever dug up a dead body before, especially one that had been in the ground for seventy-four years. Silently we were wondering what he would look like after so much time had passed. I'm sure the kids envisioned a mummy with wrinkled decaying skin, wearing rotten buckskin clothing and lying in a wooden box. To some the idea may have seemed too morbid for a bunch of twelve-year-old kids; but to us, it was pure adventure. I mean, how many junior high school kids ever get to do such a thing? It's the stuff you only read in books; right? Whatever was going on in those kids' heads at the time, they would soon be personally viewing the truth about Johnston's condition. We pulled off the 405 Freeway and turned into the Veteran's Cemetery parking lot right on schedule.

Katie parked the car and we stepped out, looking for directions to a reception office located in the Sawtelle administrative building. We hesitated for a minute or two in anticipation of what was to come and headed towards the big front doors. I remember how the kids all had huge smiles on their faces and how they all looked so grown up for their age. I did instruct them to dress appropriately, as if attending a funeral or wedding, and I felt very proud of them. Jackie wore a white party dress, Sally had on a blue dress, and Pat was outfitted with bright red jacket his mother must have purchased especially for the occasion. I told them it would be important to show respect for the process of disinterment, and that the media planned on being there as well. I also told them we needed to keep a low profile and exercise sensitivity regarding Theodore Nick and the folks at the Veterans Administration. Nick was the superintendent of the cemetery; the one who was reluctantly carrying out Rufus Wilson's orders. I personally wore a sports coat and tie which wasn't out of character for teachers. In those days ties were required dress code on a daily basis for men.

We entered the office and immediately sensed a strange coolness that had nothing to do with the temperature. Something definitely was going on behind the scenes. Although we couldn't put our fingers on it, whatever it was, it felt really uncomfortable. I instructed the kids to sit down and walked to the receptionist's desk, announcing who we were and why we had come.

"Hello," I said in a quiet, respectful tone. "My name is Tri Robinson. I'm a teacher from Park View Junior High School and my students and I are here to attend the disinterment of John Johnston."

"Yes," said the woman who greeted us not so warmly. "I know who you are and we have been expecting you." She gazed over at the students and said in a voice loud enough for them to hear, "You guys have been making quite a disturbance around here these past few days." Then she told us to take a seat and said someone would be coming along to escort us to the gravesite.

The kids did as they were told and we waited, trying to maintain our excitement. We waited for nearly an hour and no one came. This made me nervous considering the difficulties and the craziness of the last few days. I sat and made small talk with the kids until I couldn't take it any longer.

Taking Things into Our Own Hands

Earlier that year, I had stopped by the cemetery to visit Johnston's grave so I knew approximately where it was located in respect to the thousands of other identical marble grave stones. I excused myself from Katie and the students, telling them I'd be right back. I slipped outside to do a little reconnaissance. Sure enough, the moment I stepped around the corner of the building I saw a backhoe starting to dig up the ground in the exact spot I thought Johnston would be. It upset me to think they would cause my students to miss a historical event that they had been so responsible to make happen.

I went straight back into the waiting room and secretly beckoned our little group to follow me. I didn't want to draw any attention but that wasn't too difficult since the place had about as much life as a morgue. As soon as we were outside and alone, I told them to quietly follow me. I reminded them how fearful the Veterans Administration had been concerning publicity and how they wanted the disinterment event to fly under the radar so as not to create more controversial publicity. The three kids were respectful and responsive; getting caught up in the drama of the moment, they followed me in silence.

There was a helicopter from NBC circling overhead, obviously trying to film the gravesite from the air. We later learned that they'd come to the front gate earlier that morning with a film crew and had been turned away. They were told adamantly that media would not be permitted on the premises. It appeared the cemetery couldn't control the airspace however, so they had their work crew erect an awning to cover the gravesite.

Walking across the cemetery grounds I expected to be stopped at any moment. But, the moment never came. Nearing the site the first thing we observed was that the gravestone had been pulled up and the jaws of the backhoe were already digging through the sod. Two workers stood off to one side leaning on their shovels. Not far away a long black funeral hearse had backed up in preparation to receive Johnston's remains. They had unloaded a new coffin constructed of plywood which would serve as a temporary transport box. We stood at a respectful distance silently observing as the machine continued to slowly dig deeper and deeper into the earth. Then I realized my dad had joined our small delegation. Somehow knowing he was there gave me great comfort.

After many tense moments of digging, large pieces of the original casket lid were being ripped out of the hole. I couldn't believe what I was seeing. This was a historical excavation, an archaeological dig, and yet it was happening with such haste that caution of any kind was being thrown to the wind. Angered, I stepped out in front of the large machine and yelled for the operator to stop. Thankfully he did, and I walked over and peered into the hole. There were remnants of bone mixed with tarnished pewter hardware that had decorated what was once an ornate redwood casket. The backhoe had already ripped off a beautiful coffin handle which was lying on a dirt mound near the gaping hole. I was furious, but rather than making a spectacle I took up a shovel, handed my sports coat to the students and jumped into the hole, tie and all.

Discovering Johnston's Remains

I dug as carefully as I could through the wreckage, finding a few pieces of bone which were still fairly intact – a femur, a humerus, a few teeth and a large piece of Johnston's cranium. I found buttons from the military jacket he had been buried in, and other pieces of the pewter coffin parts. The casket had been locked with ornate pewter keys. There were two of them, and from the other side of the hole I located two large hinges. Judging from the artifacts we found, it was obvious to us that the military had spared no expense in Johnston's burial ceremony. The pewter parts were ornately cast with relief images of leaves and acorns and fancy scroll work. The truth is, however, there wasn't much left of Johnston himself. The cemetery was very near sea level and the water table was high. Everything had been badly decomposed. As I removed some of the larger pieces of redwood boards which had been the main planks of Johnston's casket, they came out of the ground permeated with water and felt like sponges. As I handed them up to the students and they were exposed to the open air, the planks immediately began to crumble into small fragments, and in some cases, literally turned to dust.

The workers, who by then had jumped in to help, provided plastic bags. The three students, joined by my dad, began carefully gathering what was left of Johnston's remains, bagging them for protection. They also collected the pewter hardware from the casket as well. The dirt that had caved into the old box was laced with Johnston's bone dust and fragments too small to be collected in bags. Not knowing what else to do, we carefully heaped it into a neat pile on a sheet of plywood until we felt confident we had gathered as much of Johnston's remains as we possibly could. The disinterment may not have been as romantic as we envisioned it to be, but it had been a success.

The attendants from the hearse carried the new plywood transport casket to the graveside whereby the three students shoveled the dirt laced with Johnston's bone fragments into the box. With reverent care they placed plastic bags of bone, uniform buttons and pewter coffin parts into the container. The box was already getting heavy when the two workers included the headstone. The headstone, solid marble, was approximately six feet long and weighed more than what had already been placed into the new coffin.

The long hearse moved closer to the excavation site so the heavy box didn't have to be carried any farther than was absolutely necessary. Everyone present joined in to help. Even with the workers, my dad, the students and me all lifting together, we barely got the load into the back of the vehicle. Realizing how incredibly heavy the box had become, I started to worry that the airlines would question the load and be unwilling to accept it as cargo. I wondered just what we would do if they refused to carry it.

When the work was done and the casket was ready for transport, my dad was standing by my side. He cleared his throat and then said under his breath, "You know, Tri, I don't know if I would trust those guys to get Johnston on the plane. You have way more invested in this project than they do. I'm not sure they'll fight hard enough to assure he makes that flight; especially if the airline balks at the weight."

"What do you think I should do?" I asked.

He contemplated the question for a minute then he said, "I think if it was me, I'd follow that hearse to the loading dock at LAX and check him in myself. You don't want any more mishaps this late in the game."

"You're right," I said, realizing our job wouldn't be finished until Johnston was safely loaded and on his way back to the Big Sky country.

Flying Johnston Home

As the big black van pulled away I told Katie, Pat, Jackie and Sally to get to the car as fast as they could. The car was parked several hundred yards away. Everyone, feeling the same sense of urgency, hurried to the parking lot. We didn't want to let the hearse get out of our sight. Katie, being caught up in the drama, gunned her big car's engine and left the parking lot, squealing the tires as the massive car accelerated through the cemetery's front gates. She caught Johnston's escort vehicle just as it was turning up the on-ramp of the 405 Freeway. The three kids in the backseat were cheering her on, motivated by the clear fact we were on a mission of justice.

As I recall, traffic was light that time of day, and within twenty minutes we were driving up to the airport's freight terminal without anyone questioning us at the front gate. Johnston's hearse was backing up to a loading dock while we located a parking spot nearby. As we approached the cargo bay a large rollup door opened. Out walked an official looking man with a pencil stuck behind his ear and holding a clip board. "So this is the famous Liver-eating Johnston we've all been hearing so much about," he said. "He sure has caused a stir; people have been calling here all morning just to make sure he made his flight to Billings on time."

"Really?" I asked. "What people have been calling?"

"Your folks from Montana," he responded. "They must be pretty excited about getting him up there."

Interesting, I thought. Who could that have been? Bob Edgar wasn't from Montana, but then possibly the man got his facts wrong. Bob had decided to fly Johnston's remains to Billings because the airport in Cody at that time wasn't large enough for a full sized commercial jet to land. Billings is about seventy miles north of Cody, just across the Wyoming-Montana border. Maybe Bob was already there waiting for the plane's arrival, though I thought it was highly unlikely.

"We don't really have any people in Montana," I finally said. "Could you guys hold off for a minute before unloading him? I'd like to make a quick phone call and check on a few things."

"Sure," the guy said. "The flight won't be leaving for several hours; there's no big rush."

Seeing a pay phone not far off I searched my pockets for some spare change. Long distance calls in those days, especially on pay phones, weren't cheap. My search revealed I was way short on change. In a state of desperation I turned to Katie and the kids for help. Everyone dug until we came up with a couple of bucks worth of quarters, dimes and nickels. We worked together to drop the coins into the phone and I dialed information to get Old Trail Town's number.

We put in nearly all the change we had, hoping that by some great miracle Bob would be near his phone. He answered it on the second or third ring. I talked as fast as I could, not wanting the few minutes we had to run out.

"Bob!" I said in an urgent voice. "Did you by any chance call LAX this morning to check on Johnston's flight to Billings?"

"No," he came back. "Why do you ask? What's going on?"

So I told him what the attendant had said and how it caused me to wonder. Bob kind of laughed and I could tell he was thinking about what I'd said.

"By golly," he finally responded. "I was kind of worried about this. I heard a rumor those people from Red Lodge who call themselves "Friends of John J. Johnston" were going to get a court order to stop the body from crossing the state line into Wyoming. I'll bet that's what this is all about."

This was a new revelation to me; I hadn't heard of this group before. So I asked Bob what he thought we should do. He told me to change the flight from going into Billings, Montana, to Casper, Wyoming, instead. He said he'd drive down and retrieve Johnston's remains with his pickup. He also told me to tell the airlines to keep the change of plans confidential. With that the operator came on saying my time was up; our conversation was ended.

Things around airports were much different in the '70s than they are today. There was no such thing as security, and in fact all the rules were very relaxed. That was a lucky thing for our Johnston cause. When the guys tried to pull the casket out of the back of the hearse they couldn't budge it.

"Wow," the attendant said," What the heck is in this box?"

"It's Liver-eating Johnston," I said. "He was a *very* large man."

I didn't actually lie; he was a big man. They say he may have weighed 250 pounds and was possibly six foot six inches tall. It surprised me the guy actually believed me, and rather than question me further, called for some more help to unload the huge box. He was a good-natured man and when I told him about the change of destination, he was okay with it. Even when I told him Bob Edgar would pay for it on arrival in Casper, he didn't even bat an eye. Boy, how times have changed!

By the time we made our way back to Lancaster, the school day was finished. Even so, many of the kids from the class had stuck around, as well as Linda Kiel and Chris Wangsgard. They were all anxiously waiting to hear what had transpired during our excursion. We gave a full report which provided me a much needed opportunity to debrief such an intense day. It was such a victory to know Johnston was headed to his final burial grounds after so much struggle and conflict. I couldn't help but feel a sense of deep relief and satisfaction. I thanked Katie for all she had done that day and then I headed home feeling emotionally wrung out.

It would be ten more days before we traveled back to LAX to board our flight for Wyoming. It was a very long ten days too, knowing that so much was in the works politically and legally to stop the reburial from taking place. Bob did drive to Casper and secretly collected Johnston's casket. He returned to Cody and hid the casket in someone's basement. I called him the next day just to make sure things had gone all right and he gave me the run down on what had actually transpired.

Conspiracy at the Hootie Owl Saloon
– Bear Creek, Montana

Sure enough, a delegation of Montana people had been waiting at the Billings airport for a body that never arrived. This only served to make them all the more committed to their cause. Their scheme had failed which stirred up a hornets' nest in a whole new way. The Red Lodge citizens group calling themselves "Friends of John J. Johnston" was organized by a guy named Harry Owens. They had been meeting on a regular basis, most likely every night just after five o'clock, at the Hootie Owl Saloon in Bear Creek. Each evening they would take up a collection to raise money to retain a Montana attorney named Michael J. Alterowitz. He filed a lawsuit on their behalf in the Billings Federal District Court, which contested the authority of the Veterans Administration to allow a bunch of twelve-year-old kids from California to move Johnston's remains to Old Trail Town. This naturally shook up Rufus Wilson, even more than before, especially since Johnston's body was already being hidden in someone's private basement in Cody. Rufus called Congressman Teno Rorcalio, a democrat from Wyoming, and John Melcher, the congressman from Montana who was also a democrat. It was an attempt to try to work things out as everyone was feeling the tension. Dozens of nasty letters to the editor were being submitted to newspapers all across the country. People were taking sides and being vocal about it. At one point Rufus Wilson was quoted in a paper as saying, "I don't know what I have ever done to deserve all the conflict."

Poor, poor Rufus. I'm sure he regretted the day Dick Keelor offered to take him to lunch and convinced him to do a nice thing on behalf of some seventh graders. I personally felt sorry for him because in trying to do a good thing, he had nearly started a battle all over again much like Custer's Last Stand just north of the Wyoming-Montana border. I imagine it might get a bit dangerous when people in a place like the Hootie Owl Saloon get too worked up. It brings to mind a well-known line from the old movie, *Butch Cassidy and the Sundance Kid* – *"Guns or knives, Butch?"*

Meanwhile, with only ten days to go, the verdict was still out if Johnston was going to rest in peace in the country where he had desired to be buried. As of yet, there was no peace anywhere, certainly not amongst my students at Park View School.

CHAPTER 9

Johnston Laid to Rest

That particular year the first week of June was actually the last week of school. Normally, that last week is fairly non-productive as students and teachers alike tend to get a bad case of summer fever. Usually the kids have a hard time focusing on school due to thinking about little else than the two months of freedom they are about to experience. As an antidote, most teachers would save their final testing for that week, using it as a means of getting students to stay focused right up to the last bell. For us, though, this was the culmination of two semesters of anticipation and preparation. For us, this was the most important week of the entire year. On the following Friday our delegation of eight would be heading for LAX to board a plane bound for Wyoming. If all went according to plan, the representatives for the Committee (Russ Gilliam, Eric Radzik, Ann Willey, Kelly Daugherty, Becky Carey, Lia Miller and I) would be meeting up with Chuck Johnston at the airport before flying into West Yellowstone.

All week long the media was announcing by newspaper and news reports that the on-again, off-again reburial event was going to take place the following Saturday. A good portion of our week together was spent in final preparation for our departure. We also took the time to write 'thank you' letters to all the people who had believed in us and helped to make our dream come to pass. We did this beforehand, knowing we would never get to it after the class dispersed for the summer.

A Delegation for Wyoming

It was a long week of waiting, filled with much anticipation for our departure from Los Angeles International Airport. Finally, the day arrived and there was excitement in the air. On Friday, June 7th, we loaded into some of the parents' cars and headed to LAX for the second time as a delegation for The Committee for the Reburial of Liver-eating Johnston.

For some of the students it was their first time to fly in an airplane which added an additional element to the adventure. Unlike the security at airports today, there were no security barriers and everyone could go to the boarding gates to say good bye. Of course all the parents did just that. It was a great send-off party and everyone got to meet Chuck Johnston in person for the first time.

"Are you really Liver-eating Johnston's nephew?" the students asked.

"Well, I'm pretty sure I am," responded Chuck. "At least my dad told me I was the whole time I was growing up."

While most of the kids were awkwardly trying to make conversation with Chuck, Eric Radzik stood at a distance checking him out. He held his chin with one hand as if in deep contemplation. Eric had taken very seriously his appointment as the committee's chairman and had also taken a special interest in Johnston's life.

Watching him I knew he was scrutinizing Chuck's claim to kinship. After what seemed a long time he spoke so the others had no trouble hearing him, "Yep! He is; he's related to the Liver-eater. I'm sure of it. He looks just like the picture all right."

With his pronouncement of approval something broke in the awkwardness that often accompanies kids' efforts to establish new friendships. It allowed all the students to relax and accept Chuck as one of them. As for me, I knew the picture Eric was referring to. We had the old portrait of Johnston in our class for much of the year, and in my mind it made him look like a wild-eyed crazy man straight from the wilderness. It was an old black and white picture of the Liver-eater in his mountain man heyday, cradling an old Spencer rifle in his arms, with beard and hair wildly awry. I remember wondering what Chuck might think if he knew these kids equated him with the image Eric was referring to. I thought he might take offense, but on the contrary, Chuck looked totally pleased to be authenticated by Eric and fully endorsed by the class.

Crisis in Yellowstone

We departed L.A. on a beautiful warm June morning and descended into the West Yellowstone airport in spitting snow and rain. The change of geography alone made the students realize they had entered a whole new world; a world that had helped to mold Johnston into the man he became. Leaving the plane and entering the small air terminal, I immediately spotted a row of newspaper racks near the front entrance. I asked Chuck and the kids to wait for the baggage while I went over to check out the headlines. Nearly every paper posted front-page articles concerning the reburial ceremonies. West Yellowstone is located on the corner of all three Big Sky states: Idaho, Montana and Wyoming. There were papers representing all three. I was shocked and disheartened when I read the headlines for every single one. Each held a title stating something like "Johnston not to be buried as planned tomorrow" or "The reburial of Jeremiah Johnston now postponed".

While the delegation stood by excitedly waiting for their bags, I purchased several papers and started to read them quickly. I was attempting to understand what had gone wrong. From what I could gather, it appeared that the Red Lodge group, "Friends of John J. Johnston", had actually been victorious in obtaining legal action to stop the reburial. Chuck and the kids retrieved the bags and were waiting for me when I dejectedly walked towards them. As they saw the expression on my face and the folded papers I held under my arm, they immediately knew something was wrong. The teenage giddiness quickly faded and they stood motionless, waiting for an explanation. "Well," I said trying not to sound too alarming. "These papers are indicating there has been another hitch. It doesn't look certain, but it's possible the reburial tomorrow may get postponed."

"What! No way! They can't do that! Can they?" Their outburst, a plethora of words, came out in the form of denial, appeal and question.

"Hold on!" I said. "I'm sure it will be all right; but according to what I've been reading the final decision is being made by a judge right now as we stand here."

"How can that be after all we've done?" they erupted again; "We need to get down there and speak to that judge ourselves!" Then they paused and said in a pleading sort of a way, "Mr. Robinson, can't you do something?"

"Remember, you guys, it's not over until it's over," I said. "Don't forget how many obstacles we've already overcome; and we did overcome every one. The only thing we can do now is pick up our rental car and head on over to Cody and find out the results of the decision. There's nothing we can do about it in the interim, so we might as well enjoy the drive through Yellowstone Park. You guys may not get the chance to see sites like Old Faithful again for a long time."

We located the car rental building and discovered the vehicle they reserved for us looked like an oversized station wagon, probably the forerunner for today's passenger van. Everyone loaded in as we headed for the famous Geyser Basin where the kids would see Old Faithful for the first time.

Western Airlines had flown us into West Yellowstone for the sole purpose of letting the class see the country Johnston had roamed. It was meant to be a rich time of sightseeing but with the weather dreary and the day so gloomy our appetites as tourists had been curbed. As distracted as I felt by the new development, I knew I had to put all my attention on the road ahead. The drizzling rain quickly turned to snow as we left Yellowstone Lake and climbed over the 8,541 foot Sylvan Pass on our way to the east entrance of the park. We had driven through the Geyser Basin and even saw a Grizzly bear with her two cubs on the side of the road. Still none of this took our minds off what was transpiring at that very moment in Cody. We arrived there in the later part of the afternoon, pulling into Trail Town's graveled parking lot in the persistent rain.

The first person we saw was Roy Neil. His big smile brought a refreshing glimmer of hope to our nagging feelings of despair. I rolled down my window to greet him, and he stuck his head all the way in to welcome the students. I'm sure he must have interpreted the forlorn expressions on our faces because the first words that came out of his mouth were, "You guys don't have to worry; Johnston is going to be buried here tomorrow."

Those few simple words brought such a sense of relief that an audible sigh could be heard from inside the vehicle. Everyone piled out and gathered around Roy, anxiously waiting for more details.

He could see our anticipation and went on, "It was a little uncomfortable here earlier today as we waited for the court's ruling. In the end, the judge ruled Johnston could be reinterred here tomorrow. He said that due to everyone's hard work, and because of the money which has already been invested by the Edgars and your class, we can go ahead with the reburial." Then he added, "Red Lodge may get permission to move him again later if they win the court battle, but I think it's very doubtful that will happen."

Roy Neil saved the day again simply by speaking some hopeful words. Together, we walked on into Trail Town where we found Bob Edgar waiting for us. How exciting it was for the kids to finally meet him face to face. Bob looked every bit the person they had envisioned; he was tall and lean with a dark black beard and a weathered cowboy hat which looked like he'd worn since the day he was born. He was a soft-spoken man and warmly greeted the kids, shaking each one's hand. They were finally there; standing in Old Trail Town with everything they had dreamed of now in place, ready to become a complete reality in less than twelve hours.

Red Carpet in Cody

The rain continued throughout the night. We checked into the Big Bear Motel after a strenuous day of travel and our visit to Old Trail Town. We fully expected to pay for our rooms, but were informed right away that our stay would be on the house for as long as we were in Cody. The same thing happened the evening before at the famous Buffalo Bill's Irma Hotel. They wouldn't let us pay for the dinner we ate there. And again when we had breakfast the next morning at the Pancake House. Cody had rolled out the red carpet for our small cavalcade of nine.

After breakfast on Saturday, I wanted the students to see the famous Buffalo Bill Historical Center as part of their Big Sky experience before heading to Trail Town. There, too, our money was refused for the normal admission fees. The town of Cody had gone all out to honor our students for the efforts they had made.

We arrived back at Trail Town just before noon and things

there were already bustling with activity. When Bob and his wife, Terry, saw we'd arrived, they called us aside and invited us to join them in the Old Trail Town Museum. It was here that Johnston's remains had been removed from his temporary plywood box and transferred into a handcrafted casket made by a Cody craftsman who used pine planks milled from local timber. In order to switch caskets, the temporary box had been secretly transported that morning from its basement hiding place to Trail Town.

From the time we'd arrived in Cody the evening before, I'd been looking for a moment to get Bob alone. I had a special favor to ask of him and seeing my chance there by the new casket, I pulled him aside. "Hey, Bob" I said, "I've got something to show you and a special favor to ask."

"Sure, Tri" he said. "Whatever it is, I'd be more than happy to oblige. Anything you want after all you guys have done for Cody this past year. What is it?"

Even while he was speaking, I pulled out my old Bowie knife from under the new western cut sports coat Nancy had purchased for me especially for the occasion.

"Now that's what I call a knife!" Bob said with a bit of surprise in his voice. "Where did you find that?"

I held out the large bone-handled knife, flipping it in my hand so he could take it handle first. "I've had it most of my life." I responded. "It's always been kind of special to me and I was wondering if you thought it would be okay to set it in the casket alongside of Johnston's remains? I guess it's my way of thanking Johnston for giving my class such a rich experience." Then I added. "Not only that, but by burying it with him, it might help keep me out of trouble."

He didn't know the story of my inappropriate classroom etiquette, but smiled a kind of sly, knowing smile as he said he would be happy to do it.

The Edgars were humble people. In the midst of so much media attention they had a way of remaining low key and behind the scenes. Not once during the entire day did they take any recognition for an event that never would have happened without them. In addition to the Edgars' efforts, it didn't take a genius to recognize how many others had jumped in to help orchestrate the events of that day as well. Nobody could have imagined that two thousand people would attend the reburial ceremony, making it the largest burial service in the history of Wyoming. It was a true lifesaver to have people with enough foresight and leadership ability to take responsibility for the logistics that were needed.

One of those people was a lady named May Ballinger. May was the president of the Park County Historical Society, which in a place like Cody, was a significant role. I wouldn't have even known who she was had it not been for another one of those happenstance encounters the day before. It transpired just as we were about to board our plane in Los Angeles.

While we were waiting for our plane and getting acquainted with Chuck, a young flight attendant approached the class. She saw our group and guessed who we were right away. She walked up to us and asked if we were the students going to Cody. When we acknowledged that we were, she introduced herself as May's daughter. At the time, it seemed like just a meeting of chance. When she shared about all that had been going on in Cody to prepare for the reburial ceremony, and how hard her mother and others had been working to get things ready, it gave us a new perspective. Her friendly and informative comments made us realize we weren't the only ones who had poured sweat and blood into seeing this quest become victorious. That brief encounter was humbling for us as we gratefully realized how the citizens of Cody were preparing for not only our arrival but the ceremony to come.

Redford Meets the Class

For a few more minutes we stood quietly by Johnston's casket. We contemplated all that had taken place up until this very long awaited moment. Suddenly we heard a commotion stirring outside. We peered out the windows, observing news people running back and forth preparing their camera crews for something. All three of the major networks were there: NBC, CBS and ABC. As we looked through the small-paned windows, we wondered what was going on. Then someone entered the building and gave Bob a message. Bob turned to the kids and told them Robert Redford and his twelve-year-old son, Jamie, had just arrived. He then turned to the door and promptly left. He returned in a matter of minutes, escorting the Redfords into the museum and out of the view of demanding cameras. They had arrived on a chartered Leer Jet along with a Warner Bros. publicity person. When Redford realized how much media would be present at the reburial he informed his co-worker before he got off the plane that he didn't want his presence to in any way upstage the students. For that very reason, Bob Edgar brought him straight in to meet the students. It blessed me to see how warm and friendly Redford was with them; and how happy he seemed to just hang out and spend time with them. His casual manner made the kids relax and really enjoy the short but meaningful visit they had.

Encountering Timber Jack Joe and Friends

An hour before the ceremony was to start we left the solitude of the museum and walked out onto the streets. They were filling up with people that had arrived for the ceremony. Among the regular looking folks, there was a large group of fur and leather-clad mountain men, part of a group called the American Mountain Man Association. These particular men had come from Ogden, Utah and were there to participate as pallbearers in the ceremony. They were not only authentically dressed, but carried muzzle-loading black powder rifles which would later be shot off in unison as a final salute to Johnston.

One of these mountain men stood out from all the others. He not only looked the part with his long gray beard and weathered buckskin attire, but there was something about his mannerism that set him apart. He called himself Timber Jack Joe, and, according to Bob, he lived by himself in the mountains of Wyoming near the Yellowstone Plateau. He made his livelihood by trapping and also selling artwork he had created.

Timber Jack Joe approached the students, holding two furry animals and wearing a cap that stunk of fresh skunk. The girls, not wanting him to get too close, stepped behind me and tried to become invisible and stay out of his direct path. He had a twinkle in his eye and a raccoon and red fox nestled in his arms. With a bit of mischief in his voice he said, "Hey, you kids, come over here and meet my two friends. They've been anxious to meet you after all you've done for their friend, the Liver-eater."

He was gentle enough, but it took Ann, Kelly, Becky and Lia several minutes to get over their uncertainty. Growing up in Southern California, they'd never encountered anything like this. They watched cautiously as he handed his two pets to a comrade nearby and removed a large rawhide satchel that had been hanging from his neck.

Timber Jack opened the satchel and removed a rolled up animal hide that was bound with a leather thong. He held it out for the boys to take as his voice turned to a tone of authentic sincerity, "I want you kids to have this as a token of my personal appreciation for all you have done to make this happen here today."

There was no question about it; this man was a character and obviously a well-known personality around Cody. As his countenance softened the students sensed he was more than an old man looking for a reaction. They decided at once that they liked him. One of the boys took the package and gingerly untied the leather string, carefully unrolling its contents. Whatever it was, it had been made from an antelope hide that still had its fur on one side. A closer examination revealed that on the back side was a hand painted self-portrait of Timber Jack Joe himself. It truly was an amazing work of art.

As we stood there appreciating the gift we were given, Timber Jack Joe went on, "I want to honestly thank you kids for all your efforts," he said. "You have treated us mountain men and the folks here in the Big Sky country with respect and dignity. You have done a great justice to the history and the memory of the people who inhabited and settled this land."

Johnston's Reinterment: How It Happened

The reburial procession started just before two o'clock, right on schedule. Bob Edgar directed the procession himself, walking from the old museum building and on down the main street of Trail Town. Timber Jack Joe led the way, mounted on an old white horse. He was followed by five buckskinned pallbearers and Robert Redford, who together carried Johnston's casket. The casket was covered with an American flag and a large evergreen wreath made of juniper and wildflowers that the students had gathered in the hills earlier that morning. As the procession came to the new gravesite, the casket was carefully set over the deep hole lined with logs. Wooden poles supported the box over the freshly dug grave.

A Sioux minister named Godfrey Broken Rope was the first to speak. Though I don't remember his exact words, I do recall they were powerful and moving. Robert Redford was next. He said nothing about himself or the role he had played in the movie, *Jeremiah Johnson,* which personified Johnston as a mountain man legend. Instead, he honored the students for their diligence, tenacity and hard work. He said, "The world should look out for kids like these because they could take over the world if they put their minds to it." Then he added, "And maybe that wouldn't be so bad." It was short but very empowering and gratifying, especially for the kids who were standing next to him.

Next, Kelly Daugherty spoke. Kelly represented our class, and I have no record of what she actually said. What I do remember is how proud I was of her for standing in front of so many cameras and people, knowing her words would be broadcast over three major networks.

The flag was removed from the casket, folded and handed to Robert Frisby, a uniformed member of Cody's American Legion. He, in turn, presented it to our small delegation who received it with gratitude and reverence. With that, the mountain men shot off a dramatic volley from their muzzle loaders as a final salute to Johnston. The casket was then lowered by ropes into the grave. As a bugler began to play taps into the crisp mountain air, I couldn't help but look up to Heart Mountain in the far distance. It struck me then that the rain had stopped just as the ceremony procession began. Now, rays of sunlight were streaming through the broken clouds, casting a soft light on the western hills. It was the perfect finish to a school year; a year that would not be soon forgotten.

As the Sun Over Trail Town Was Setting

The crowd started to thin out by three o'clock and completely dissipated soon after. The only ones left were those who had played integral roles in making the day a success. Robert Redford and his son had left to fly home to Utah after only one mishap. Jamie gave his dad a real scare when he had temporarily gotten lost in the crowd at the end of the ceremony. It was only a matter of minutes before his dad located him, but it clearly gave Robert an uncomfortable moment of anxiety.

Without anyone intentionally making it happen, Bob Edgar, Chuck Johnston, all seven of the students, and I spontaneously congregated beside Johnston's gravesite. The sun was just starting to set and the changing light reflecting off the clouds in the western skyline was magnificent. For a long time we just stood there together in silence. Words couldn't express what any of us were feeling; trite conversation seemed out of place. The silence we experienced seemed reverent, and came with a sense of awe mixed with deep satisfaction and relief. I remember not wanting to break the magic of the moment. At the same time I didn't want it to slip away, or get lost in the rest of the events that night. I felt it was important for the students to verbalize what was in their hearts at that moment, preserving that special time forever.

So, I asked two simple questions; "What are you guys thinking? What are you feeling?"

I forget who actually started, but their thoughts came out with amazing clarity and sincerity in a way that is rare for a twelve-year-old. One by one, they spontaneously shared what the day had meant. One by one, my students revealed heartfelt emotion with tears in their eyes. It was a rare moment in the life of a teacher; a moment I couldn't have made happen. It was a moment that made all the planning, all the work, all the frustration and anxiety worth it. As I sit now, recounting the events of a day that happened over forty years ago, I feel immense gratitude in my heart for such an amazing experience. I even remember the thunder and lightning, flashing and rumbling miles away in the Yellowstone, which only served to enhance that special time, etching it indelibly on my mind.

As our time of solitude came to an end, Chuck and the students headed off to find Timber Jack Joe who had invited them for dinner at the mountain men encampment. When they were gone, Bob and I were left standing alone. I noticed him peering into the deep hole, looking thoughtfully down at Johnston's casket.

I could almost read his thoughts and said, "You're worried about someone getting permission to dig him up someday, aren't you?"

"Yep," he said, "that thought had crossed my mind."

"You know, Bob," I said; "I had a thought, too."

"What's that?" he asked, looking up curiously.

"Well," I continued. "I was remembering how I read about the way they buried Buffalo Bill's body in Colorado, and how it was a similar situation to what's going on here. The people of Wyoming had threatened to dig him up and bring him back to his own town of Cody."

"Yep; you're right," he said. "That is true."

"Well, do you remember what the Colorado folks did?" I asked.

"Yeah," he responded with a bit of mischief in his eye. "They filled his grave with concrete."

"Right," I stated. "Why don't we do the same?"

Bob laughed and said, "I wonder if it's too late to get it done tonight?"

As it turned out, it wasn't. Bob called the local cement company who knew as well as anyone in Cody what had happened that day. They brought a full load of wet concrete and dumped it all in the hole until it was filled to the top. Bob then stuck a bleached buffalo skull in the wet cement and left it to dry. And so it is, that Liver-eating Johnston's few bone fragments along with my old Bowie knife will forever remain in the small graveyard of Old Trail Town along with six other Wyoming legends: Belle Drewry (Wyoming homesteader, 1867-1897), Jack Stilwell (Frontiersman, 1850-1903), Jim White (Buffalo Hunter, 1828-1880) W. A. Gallagher and Blind Bill (Wyoming cowboys, murdered in 1894) and Phillip Vetter (Killed by a grizzly bear, 1855-1892).

Meanwhile, the students joined Timber Jack Joe at the

mountain men's encampment for a very unusual dinner. That night they enjoyed eating delicacies I'm sure they'd never tasted before or probably since. The meal consisted of roasted beaver, fried antelope and elk livers (an appropriate dish), bear stew and fresh trout. Everything had been smoked and cooked over an open fire. It was a unique feast with some lively characters that was not soon to be forgotten by some very happy kids.

CHAPTER 10

Trail's End

Today, a monument stands proudly at the site of Johnston's relocated grave. On top of a natural rock foundation is a large bronze statue of a mountain man mounted on his striding horse. The monument, holding the noble position at the head of Johnston's grave, is surrounded by a rustic iron fence. Placed at the foot of the grave is the veteran's marble gravestone that once marked Johnston's original California grave for seventy-four years. Just outside the rustic fence, resting on the top of a smaller rock pedestal, is a plaque commemorating the day in 1974 that Johnston was reinterred into his Wyoming grave. The words inscribed on the plaque give recognition and honor to twenty-four 7th grade students from Park View Junior High School who dared to believe John "Liver-eating" Johnston could get his last wish. Currently, those students are scattered across the country, separately living out their lives. But, they will remain forever united through the fulfillment of a dream they once shared together.

I moved on as well. After ten more years of teaching at Park View Junior High, I entered the full-time ministry. Upon resignation of my position with the school district, I worked eight more years in Lancaster as associate pastor of a non-denominational Christian church called the Desert Vineyard. It was a difficult and soul-searching decision to give up my teaching job; a career that had been so rewarding. But, Nancy and I both knew it was time for us to take another risk, and so we moved on to a new chapter in our life.

In 1989, we left our mountain home in Southern California. It was also difficult leaving the old family ranch after nearly twenty years of living there and raising our family in its rustic beauty and solitude. We found it very hard to leave behind so many cherished memories and the rich friendships we'd developed. Nancy and I felt it was time to return to Idaho, where our life together began. This time we would come as a family with our two teenage kids: our daughter, Kate, and our son, Brook. We decided to begin yet a new adventure, as we committed to start a church in Boise. We planted the church with a small band of courageous people who chose to join in our venture and move with us from Lancaster, California to Idaho. The new church was called the Vineyard Christian Fellowship of Boise and it has grown through the years to a congregation of over 2,000 people.

The Return of Mr. Hanson

One morning in the mid 1990's, while working in our new church office, I received an unexpected phone call. Our staff was very small then, but I remembered the counsel I had received from my teacher, Mr. Hanson, so many years before. I had two wonderful women working for me, believing that Lori Thompson and Sharon Taylor were the fulfillment of Bill Hanson's words when he told me I would need two good secretaries to make my life a success. As I write this memoir both of them have now worked alongside me as administrative assistants for some thirty years. They are faithful co-workers who, through the years, have become more like sisters to me than employees.

Without a doubt, they have greatly contributed to whatever success I've experienced in my professional life.

As I recall that day, Sharon answered the phone in the reception area. Because we didn't have a sophisticated phone system, she put the caller on hold and walked back to the cubby hole that served as my office.

"Tri" she said, "there's a woman on the phone who says she knew you when you were a boy. I think her husband was one of your teachers."

"Really?" I responded, "I wonder who that could be. Did she say her name?"

"I think she mentioned that her name was Beverly June," Sharon stated.

"Beverly June Hanson?" I commented with surprise in my voice. Sharon noticed I was more excited than usual about getting a phone call, as she looked at me with a quizzical expression.

"That's Mr. Hanson's wife, and he's my old teacher! The one I always talk so much about from my junior high school days," I said. "How in the world do you suppose she ever located me here in Idaho?"

"I don't know," she answered. "But you might want to pick up your phone and find out. It's a long distance call."

I picked up my phone and spoke into the receiver, "Hello, this is Tri."

"Tri, this is Beverly June Hanson. How did you ever get all the way up to a place like Boise, Idaho? How are you anyway?"

I told her I was fine and gave her a short version of my pilgrimage but was more concerned why she'd gone to the trouble of finding me. I had a sinking feeling this wasn't a social call.

"What's going on, Beverly June?" I finally asked. "Why are you calling?"

Her voice became sober. "Tri" she said, "Bill is dying. He is in the late stages of Alzheimer's and doctors have informed me he only has a few weeks to live. He's had a hard fight over this last year, but it has finally gotten the best of him."

I didn't know what to say. I felt badly that Mr. Hanson was dying, but I felt worse about the fact that I hadn't taken time to go see him for years. I always intended to but life has a way of getting away from us. I had told the story so many times, to so many people, about his influence on me and how he had empowered me all those years before. But, I had never told him personally.

I responded to Beverly June, feebly saying, "I'm so sorry to hear that." Then I asked if there was anything I could do for her.

"As a matter of fact, there is." She replied. "Before Bill became incapacitated a surprising thing happened. I'm not sure where he got it; probably someone sent it to him. Somehow, he got hold of a preaching tape you had done, and I think it was somewhere in Australia."

"In Australia!" I responded. "How in the world?" I had taught in Australia several times, but in those days there was no such thing as the internet, and all teaching was recorded on cassette tapes. I couldn't imagine how it made its way back to Southern California.

"I don't know," she went on, "but, he listened to it over and over again, right up until he wasn't capable of doing so any longer. He told me to find you, no matter where you were in the world, and ask if you would come here and do his funeral."

I was honored and I told her so. I thought how ironic it was that Bill Hanson had been such a blessing to me at the beginning of my life's journey, and now I had the chance to bless him at the end of his.

A couple of weeks later I flew from Boise into LAX where

my parents picked me up and drove me into downtown Hollywood to the memorial service location. I remember feeling panicked because my plane was late, and we arrived at the funeral only minutes before the service was scheduled to start. I was quickly ushered into a back room where I met Beverly June and her two sons. I only knew them by their nicknames, Chip and Woody. I remember Chip the best as he was more my age. I heard he'd been building a reputation in the movie industry. Having just directed the film, *A River Wild,* which starred Meryl Streep and Kevin Bacon, he was well on his way to a very bright future. Curtis (his real name) Hanson went on to become a successful director, producer and screenwriter. Today, he may be best known as director and producer of the popular television series, *L.A. Confidential.*

Concerning the service for Mr. Hanson, Beverly June told me she didn't know what to expect in regards to who would be attending. She asked me to take charge of the service and do whatever I thought was best. As we entered the large room, people where still coming through the back doors of the facility, filling every empty seat that remained. The place was full of people I didn't know, but it was clear that those represented were professionals from many walks of life. I remember fighting back those familiar old feelings of inadequacy as I looked out and prepared myself to address such an intimidating crowd. I opened the service in prayer, thanking God for the gift of Bill Hanson's life and his impact on so many in the room. Then, not knowing what else to do, I shared my own story. I told them about how Bill Hanson had empowered and believed in me as a young man. Looking out across the room, I saw tears welling up in the eyes of many. Clearly, I was not alone; there were many who had experienced the memorable influence of this man.

When I finished, I invited others to share as I had done.

One after another, people stood and paid tribute as they told of their experiences which often paralleled my own. Many gave Mr. Hanson credit for his part in helping to set their compass toward the successful lives they now lived. There were authors, a poet, songwriters, teachers and journalists. The room was filled with creative people of every kind, whose lives had been inspired by this one human being; a teacher who dedicated a large portion of his life for the sake of others. His impact was like a stone thrown into a pool of still water, causing ripples to go beyond his own sphere of influence to the point of affecting some he never knew. It was an inspiration to all, and at the same time, a silent challenge to all – to go and do the same.

"The Stuff of Which Winners are Made"
As I now enter the golden years of my own life, I am acutely aware of how temporal life really is. Even in writing this account I am challenged not to waste a single day; to value each one as a great gift. That thought brings to mind one of my students, Kif Anderson. I mentioned Kif earlier as the student who wrote his personal reflections on the role he played as part of the reburial project in the book, *Chicken Soup for the Teenage Soul*. In his contribution to the book he wrote a final paragraph which is a constant reminder of the impact a teacher can have on the lives of their students. It reminded me that being in a position of influence is one not to be squandered. I was heartbroken to learn that Kif died tragically in 2012, but am deeply grateful for his words which revealed his heart on this matter.

From then on, throughout the school, our class was referred to as the 'Gravediggers.' But we preferred to think of ourselves as the 'Dream Lifters.' What we learned that year was not just about how to write effective letters, how our government works, or even what you have to get through to accomplish such a simple thing as moving a grave site. The lesson was that nothing can beat persistence. A bunch of kids at the beginning of our teenage years had made a change. We learned that we were the stuff of which winners are made." [1]

Who Really Won?

The greatest people I've known in my life have been lifetime "learners". They are those who never thought they'd fully arrived in their professions but always maintained a desire to keep growing. I've always wanted to be one of those people.

I began my teaching career in 1971, and I still recall the day Dr. Dwight Stapley hired me and handed me the key to my first classroom. It was an amazing and magical moment. I remember holding the key in the palm of my hand as I carefully examined it. Stamped on one side of the brass metal was "ROOM 14". For me, that simple key held the power to unlock the beginning of a new chapter of my life. The first day of school was only three days away. I was both scared and filled with anticipation as I wondered what would happen when Room 14 was inhabited with my first students on Monday morning.

The halls were empty and echoed with the sound of my footsteps as I approached the door that had the number "14" posted above it. I pushed the large brass key into the lock and turned it with an awareness of a lump in my throat. I slowly opened the door and stepped into a room filled with rows of empty desks and chairs. A blank bulletin board greeted me. There was an eerie silence, interrupted only by the loud ticking of a large round school clock located above the blackboards at the head of the class. I remember standing there that afternoon with pause in my heart. So, this would be the place where it

---

[1] *Chicken Soup for the Teenage Soul*, The Gravediggers of Parkview Junior High by Kif Anderson (Health Communications Inc., 1997) Pg. 298

would happen. This would be the place where I would discover if I was a teacher or not; where my six years of college preparation would, in a very real way, undergo their final exam. In just three short days a bell would ring, and students would come bounding through the door in search of a desk to call home for the next year. They would take a seat and immediately begin to evaluate their new teacher, attempting to decide if he deserved a "pass" or "fail" grade.

It struck me then, standing there in a state of shock, that nothing I'd learned in all of my education classes and graduate work had prepared me for the reality of what was about to happen. I was never told how to gain the respect of twelve-year-olds in the throes of puberty; how to handle a kid who plastered a spit wad on the face of that big round clock; or how to inspire and motivate kids to *want* to learn. I knew much about the dissemination of information, but not much about the empowerment of inspiration. I'd learned about adolescent development and the theory of learning, but not how to discover the uniqueness of a kid who didn't feel special in any way. I was never taught to do for my students what a man like Mr. Hanson had done for me. It became apparent at that moment, if success was to be attained, that the one in the classroom who would have to learn the most was me!

The year we reburied the old bones of John Liver-eating Johnston was a year of great learning. For me, it was the year I discovered how much influence a teacher can have on the lives of their students. I learned that it was a great privilege, and not one to be taken lightly. I learned that successful teaching was much like the ministry and had to be embraced as a calling more than merely a means of livelihood. I learned that real education demands the teacher go beyond objectives focused on students passing exams for the sake of moving up in the system of education. On the contrary, I discovered that the teacher who will make the greatest lifetime impact on a student's life is the one who is ready to dig deep for creative means and innovative methodologies. They are willing to sometimes take risks, going outside the norm of tradition. They provide learning experiences that challenge and reveal to a young person their own hidden gifting. They empower them with truthful words, believe in them no matter how disabled they may appear, or resistant to the learning process. All of this is the hallmark of a great teacher.

For me, the year of the "Gravediggers" was one of insight and growth. My prayer was not centered on my own growth, but rather on the lives of my students – that they would somehow be enriched by the amazing things they had experienced in my class that year at Park View Junior High School. My hope was, and is, that they learned at least a fraction of all I did. I hope they grew in their appreciation of American Literature and History, research, writing, and how things get done in this world. But, if they only learned, in the apt words of Kif Anderson, "the stuff of which winners are made," then that would be more than enough for me.

ACKNOWLEDGMENTS

Though there are many who have made an impact on me as an educator, I would like to acknowledge those who contributed to the final outcome of this amazing story and the continuing saga of this dyslexic teacher.

Chris Wangsgard, Jane Shieh, Linda Kiel, Ron Huebert and many other teachers at Park View School who not only put up with my crazy ideas, but encouraged them.

All of the Park View students, who continually challenged me to be creative and to break status quo, making my years of teaching some of the best in my life.

Mr. Bill Hanson, and the thousands of school teachers like him, who are dedicated to enriching the minds of young people while caring about their hearts and souls.

My Dad, Dr. F. W. Robinson (former Principal of Beverly Hills High School), who continued to fight against standardized education at the Idaho State Capital until age 94, when I wrestled him to the floor and took away his car keys.

Dr. Louie Attebery and Shirley Kroeger, who accepted me not only as a student but as a friend, making my time at the College of Idaho a life-enriching experience.

Robert Redford, who took the time and effort to bless and empower the students who called themselves "The Committee for the Reburial of Liver-eating Johnston"; and who, through his creative efforts, introduced Johnston as a classic American legend to the world.

Dr. Richard (Dick) Keelor (past Director of the President's Council for Physical Fitness) who, in an effort to convince Rufus Wilson to support the students from Park View School, threatened to put him in an old fashion "Liver-eating Johnston headlock" as a motivational ploy.

Rufus Wilson (Director of the Veterans Administration in the 1970's) who didn't need to be put in a headlock, and made the students of Park View School the official the honorary next of kin to John Liver-eating Johnston so they could gain the authority to dig up and move his old bones.

Chuck Johnston, the great nephew of Liver-eating Johnston and the only remaining next of kin, who went to bat for the students of Park View School and became their friend.

Bob and Terry Edgar, Old Trail Town, The Cody Historical Society, and all the wonderful folks of Cody, Wyoming who helped make Johnston's reburial ceremony a successful historical event.

The Hootie Owl Saloon in Bear Creek and all the folks of Red Lodge, Montana, who fought the good fight for Johnston's remains and in so doing, made this story a lot more fun to tell.

Lori Thompson and Sharon Taylor, two dear friends and co-workers, who have been the fulfillment of Mr. Hanson's prophetic counsel for the past thirty years of my professional life.

Nancy, my wife, who was responsible for the conflict created by the reburial of Johnston, nearly causing a war comparable to Custer's Last Stand near the Montana-Wyoming border simply by suggesting that my seventh grade class should dig up and move Johnston's body in the first place.

More from Tri Robinson

Websites to follow Tri & Nancy Robinson
- Homestead site – www.timberbuttehomestead.com
- Ministry site – www.i-61.org
- Books, position papers and leadership – www.trirobinson.org
- A website for Tri's book, *Rooted in Good Soil,* published by
  Baker Books: www.rootedingoodsoil.com

Other books by Tri Robinson:
- *Revolutionary Leadership* (Ampelon Publishing)
- *Saving God's Green Earth – Rediscovering the Church's
  Responsibility to Environmental Stewardship* (Ampelon Publishing)
- *Small Footprint, Big Handprint – How to live simply
  and love extravagantly* (Ampelon Publishing)
- *Rooted in Good Soil – Cultivating and Sustaining
  Authentic Discipleship* (Baker Books)
- *Jesus in the Mirror* (Regal)
- *Chronicles of Sustainable Homesteading*

CPSIA information can be obtained at www.ICGtesting.com
Printed in the USA
LVOW07s1749101114

412930LV00003B/188/P